WHAT READERS ARE SAYING

"*Different Doesn't Mean Broken* is a courageous exploration of self-acceptance and resilience. As a mom and founder of Free Mom Hugs, I'm moved by Don Mamone's powerful invitation to honor our true selves. This book shines a light on the beauty of authenticity and defying expectations – a heartfelt reminder that being different is a gift, not a flaw. It's a book the LGBTQIA+ community and their families can benefit from, offering insight, hope, and a path to deeper understanding and connection."

—SARA CUNNINGHAM, *Founder, Free Mom Hugs*

"If you can't read this book for yourself right now, read it for your kids. Read it for your partner. Read it for your future self who isn't ready to show up yet. This is the book you didn't know how badly you needed, until you've finished reading it."

—NIK RIGGS, *Full Spectrum Doula & Creative Entrepreneur*

"Prepare to view your own shadowy, forgotten corners as the author bleeds across the page to bring you light and guide you through your own darkness. This read was a journey, and multiple cracks formed in my carefully constructed walls throughout the process. Some were sealed with tears and hope for the future, while others were left open to allow room for future growth. An inspirational and emotionally compelling combination of poignantly relatable storytelling and purposeful guidance toward self-discovery, self-acceptance, and a deeper sense of understanding, for both yourself and your fellow humans."

—LEIGHA WOLFFE, *Author*

"This isn't just a book about one person's journey of coming out as non-binary or about gender. This book is about being true to yourself and living authentically. It's about truly seeing yourself, loving yourself, accepting yourself. And it's about all the messy things that come along with that journey."

—LEAH WEINBERG, *Attorney, Founder Chroma Law*

"Shines a light on the courage it takes to embrace one's true identity, celebrating the diversity and power of showing up authentically in a world that desperately needs to listen."

—BRIAN KENNEDY, MS, LPC, *Therapist*

"I started a list of quotes to share with my students. This book is a gift to us all."

—LEEANNE ROGERS, *Founder, Life Design with LeeAnne*

"For those who struggle with their identity – not necessarily just gender identity, but with being their own true self in whatever form that takes – this book can offer validation, solace, and strength. For those that don't necessarily struggle with identity themselves, this book can bring a better understanding of how their actions – or inactions – can greatly affect those who are struggling. Our lives can't help but be enriched when we take the time to listen and learn from others. After all, "The world can always use more mercy, empathy, and compassion."

—JOANNA NEWCOMB, *Founder, Manifest 37*

"A book on self-acceptance, families... a reminder the *cover* is only part of a *book*."

—ANDREA SMITH, *Intercultural Communication Specialist*

"For those who don't fit the stereotypical heteronormative mold, being unapologetically yourself requires immense courage and carries inherent risks. It shouldn't be this way, but it often is. Within the pages of this book, you'll discover a beautiful blueprint for taking those risks and betting on yourself. Don's work is an invaluable guide for anyone seeking a more fulfilling and wonderful life."

—HEATHER VICKERY, *Transformation Coach, Author, Podcaster*

"Every parent of an LGBTQIAS+ child should read this to gain knowledge and a better understanding of growing up different from what the world expects. I wasn't prepared to cry until I read page 75! Everyone has their own coming-out story, and it's a rebirth of who we are to ourselves and how the world will see us from that day forward. It's a release of emotions that many of us never knew we had until that moment."

—RIC SIMMONS, *DEI Educator & Publisher*

DIFFERENT DOESN'T MEAN BROKEN

Living Courageously Outside the Binary

DON MAMONE

Copyright © 2024 Don Mamone
All Rights Reserved

Year of the Book
135 Glen Avenue
Glen Rock, PA 17327

ISBN: 978-1-64649-461-3 (hardcover)
ISBN: 978-1-64649-438-5 (paperback)
ISBN: 978-1-64649-439-2 (ebook)

No part of this book may be reproduced or transmitted in any form or by any means, electronic or mechanical, including photocopying, recording or by any information storage and retrieval system without written permission from the author.

Cover artwork © "UNTITLED" used by permission, courtesy of Wingchow.

Cover photos by Awesomesauce Photography.

About the Author photo by Christa Meola Pictures.

To Emily

For seeing and accepting me when I couldn't
For loving me when I wouldn't
For protecting my wounded heart
For choosing me every day
For showing me what unconditional love truly is
For being my lobster

To Frankie

For being my reason why

To Sissy

For growing up fast so I didn't have to
For taking care of me while you were putting up with me
For being in my corner and picking me up when I get knocked down
For being my voice of reason and my shoulder to cry on
For being my sissy

To Kevin

For gently teaching me with wisdom and insight
For encouraging me to see the world through the eyes of others
For being patient, compassionate and committed
For being someone I always look to and look up to

To Dom & Aiden

For loving and accepting me without hesitation
For supporting me in your words and actions
For making me proud every day
For being the sons I never had

To Nona

For making unimaginable sacrifices for your children
For raising us to be kind, caring, and strong
For being our mom before anything else

CONTENTS

Foreword, *by Kevin Concannon* i
Introduction 1
1 | Creating Order Out of Chaos 5
2 | Identity 31
3 | The Fallout 47
4 | Letting Someone In 69
5 | Different Doesn't Mean Broken 85
6 | Coming Out 113
7 | Invisible No More 127
8 | The Windfall 141
9 | Becoming 151
10| What's Next 179
Conclusion 199

"Everybody's story is different. There's your version and my version and everything in between. But the one thing that all of those stories have in common is that moment right before you say those words when your heart is racing and you don't know what's coming next. That moment's really terrifying. And then once you say those words, you can't unsay them. A chapter has ended and a new one's begun, and you have to be ready for that."

—Dan Levy as John, *The Happiest Season*

FOREWORD

New Year's Eve 1996 will always stick in my memory. It was the first time meeting my girlfriend's family. All the questions, the looks, and the worries played through my mind as I made my way up the driveway. I thought I was prepared. Still, the many voices I heard as I approached the door made me question my resolve.

When the door opened, it appeared that I had been invited into an argument rather than a dinner. People of all ages were scattered around the threshold, some on the stairway, others around the front door, pointing at each other and talking animatedly. As best as I could piece together, my girlfriend's brother wanted to go out to a party with his friends, and his family was opposed.

Though this took the pressure off me, my girlfriend's family was telling her brother that it wasn't safe to go out, that he should stay home and visit, that life was too short. Meanwhile his friends were telling him that he needed to go, that their plans wouldn't be the same without him. In five minutes or so, the dust cleared, and my future in-laws and their friends were parked on the sofa, awaiting a night at home playing board games and eating.

While this will always live in my memory, for my future in-law, Don Mamone, it was probably an evening best forgotten, another example of struggling with people telling Don how to be, about what it means to be "safe," and about how life should be lived.

When we attempt to protect another by telling them what they should do or how they should be – presuming that we know what's best – we forget that our words can have long-term consequences and inflict potential, albeit unintended, damage.

It is natural for us to sort people we meet into categories, based on their appearance, words, and actions, but it is easy to forget that those labels do not create the actions or people. Nor do these labels define them. They are instead a response to perceived commonalities. How people are seen by us is not a natural part of who they are as human beings. By mistakenly merging these two in our minds, by "seeing" people only in terms of who they should be, problems arise and people suffer.

When I was in college, I remember seeing one of my professors at the grocery store. For some reason the very notion that they actually shopped was alarming. College professors are visualized as uncaring and forgetful about common things, so how can they also be shopping for chicken and a bottle of bourbon?

Poet John Keats suggested we adopt a perspective he labeled "negative capability," that we should always try to engage with the world as mysterious and different, and not see it through a set of predetermined ideas. In this way, we could understand others while also learning how we can understand ourselves.

It is not easy to live a life filled with Keats' sense of mystery. Strategies and systems are needed to organize daily life. This book provides ways for dealing with everyday encounters, ways to approach the journey, and to find a genuine sense of self in a world that is not always accepting.

It speaks of our intrinsic desire to feel like we belong, with the hope we will be appreciated and accepted for who we really are. In the absence of that environment, during our formative years and beyond, Don offers wisdom for how we can approach a future in which we realize we are allowed to explore our identity – without fear or judgment, either from the public at large, our loved ones, or (perhaps most damaging of all) ourselves.

FOREWORD

Thinking back on the turmoil of that night when I first met Don, and all the different voices they heard telling them what is best, it is clear they were dealing with similar voices inside of themselves every day, telling them the right way to be, to act and to appear. When they called a few years ago to tell our family something important, we didn't know what to expect. They appeared anxious on FaceTime, wrestling to hold back emotion, while saying who they truly were. I think back on our family's silence when they spoke, with the realization that Don had finally been able to overcome those voices telling him to stay inside, to stay safe, and that now he finally was able to go to that party that he missed so many years previous. In this was a mix of sadness and hope, that the challenges of social expectations, and the right way of being in the world, made it so hard for them to be their authentic self. But there is also a sense of hope that their journey – and others' journeys – can be about change, about making life better.

If you or someone close to you is struggling with matters of identity or authenticity, hoping to learn to accept yourself and others in ways that provide a solid foundation to live in this world, this book provides a pathway forward. Much more hopeful than the turmoil in which I first met Don, a different future awaits, one in which our world will be able to listen and understand the individual mystery of life.

This is a journey I hope you will want to join.

—KEVIN CONCANNON, Ph.D.

INTRODUCTION

"There is no living thing that is not afraid when it faces danger. The true courage is in facing danger when you are afraid."

—*Claudia Rankine*

This book isn't about being nonbinary. It's about being different. It's about being convinced that there's something, *anything*, about you that's not okay. Not appreciated. Not allowed. It's about embracing authenticity and rejecting conformity. It's also about my journey and my stories, so in that way, you're going to learn a little about what gender is, what it isn't, how it's experienced, and what life's like living courageously outside the gender binary. More than that though, you're going to learn that there's freedom on the other side of the fear... and that being different doesn't mean you're broken.

The idea of writing a book has been on my to-do list for a very long time. Despite my intention, life routinely got in the way. For a while, I conveniently placed the blame on things outside myself.

Emily and I were building a business. *I didn't have the time.*

Emily and I were having a baby. *I didn't have the energy.*

Emily and I own a business and we have a baby. *I didn't have the time or the energy.*

Eventually, I saw these reasons for what they really were – excuses. Yes, I was busy, and sure, I was tired, but I knew that when I was truly ready to write a book – my book – I would make the time.

At first, I think I liked the notion of being an author. I've always loved to read and I liked to write, but the idea of sitting down and composing hundreds of pages was intimidating. It seemed complicated. It isn't enough to just *write* the book. You also have to edit it, publish it, and market it in the hope that you can actually sell the book. The notion of being an author wasn't enough motivation for me to commit to all the process entailed.

However, I know now that powerful forces were holding me back… and not just from writing my book.

When I first considered the idea, I was a hospitality veteran with a decade's worth of knowledge and experience as a Director of Events in prominent Southern California hotels. I was a successful entrepreneur and business owner, recently married to a kind, creative, talented, and beautiful woman. Emily and I were partners in business and in life. We traveled the world for our loyal photography clients. We bought a home and, before long, we had a baby. By all appearances, I was confident, happy, and successful. Appearances can be deceiving. On the inside I was scared, isolated, and desperately afraid.

> *By all appearances, I was confident, happy, and successful.*

I learned at a young age that there was a set of rules I would be expected to follow, a host of things I was supposed to be, and expectations about who I would become. There was a list of things I was allowed and not allowed to do, as well as a list of things that I was and wasn't allowed to be. According to these rules, there were elements about who I was, what I wanted, and what felt right that were simply not okay.

I was ashamed of who I was and felt guilty about how I felt. Everywhere I looked and everyone I looked to confirmed that these were, in fact, the rules. My rules. And so it was. The moment I believed them was the moment I accepted them as my reality for

Introduction

the rest of my life. What I deeply wanted, what absolutely felt right, and who I truly was didn't matter.

Absent of the opportunity to be who I was, I showed the world what it wanted to see. I did what I was allowed to do. And eventually, I created the version of me that I was expected to be.

Until one day, something profound and significant happened. Someone came into my life, and in that person, I found the courage to share the part of me I had always been ashamed of. That's the moment everything changed.

On the inside I was scared, isolated, and desperately afraid.

Admittedly, life didn't change immediately. Everything didn't happen all at once, but coming out altered the trajectory of my life. With the support and encouragement of Emily and our daughter Frankie, and countless others, I found my way from self-doubt to self-acceptance. I was determined to learn to love all of me, unconditionally and without hesitation. I was committed to living a life of unapologetic authenticity.

I knew it wasn't going to be easy, but I hoped it was going to be worth it.

And it has been.

I have learned every day that the powerful forces which previously held me back no longer have control of me. I have stopped letting them keep me from being who I am, embracing what felt right, or doing what I wanted.

I finally found all the motivation I needed to do this incredibly hard thing – to write this book. It's you. You're my motivation. I'm telling you my story because I know that I'm not alone. I know I'm not the only one who's been pressured into being something I'm not. I know I'm not the only one who has surrendered what I want to fit in with what was allowed. I know I'm not the only one who did what was expected at the expense of what was possible.

Amidst all of our beautiful differences, we are united in the common desire to be the authors of our own story. We're all hoping for the freedom to tell the world who we are and the confidence to protect what we want... the conviction to defy permission and the courage to disregard expectation.

I've met some remarkable people and learned extraordinary lessons on my journey from conformity to authenticity. I learned there's freedom on the other side of fear. I learned that I'm special and unique (just like everyone else). I learned that other people's opinions are none of my business. I learned that I never need to apologize for who I am. I learned that I don't need to be fixed just because I'm different. And I learned that *different* doesn't mean *broken*.

And yet, I still ache for a world where we don't need to be courageous to be who we truly are.

> *I ache for a world where we don't need to be courageous to be who we truly are.*

Despite how far I've come and all the things I'm proud to have accomplished, I still have oodles to learn. There's also plenty I still want. I want you to believe in yourself and to know that you're enough. I want you to know that you matter and that you're valuable beyond measure. I want you to love yourself unconditionally. I want you to live your life authentically and unapologetically. More than anything though, I want you to want all of this, and more, for yourself.

Want alone won't be enough. Doing the things you were convinced were impossible will require dedication and determination. If you haven't quite found your motivation yet, maybe you're not looking in the right place. Not only is it within reach, it's closer than you may think. To find your motivation you need only look inside yourself. You are your own motivation. You will find the dedication and determination, and all the other things you need, in due time and with a little help from me.

When you're ready, I invite you to make the first move.

1
CREATING ORDER OUT OF CHAOS

"Education is thinking, and thinking is looking for yourself and seeing what's there, not what you got told was there."

—*William Least Heat-Moon*

It was 1980-something. I was five years old and in my aunt's basement playing with my sister and our cousins, as we so often did on Sundays. My grandfather and uncles were watching the Steelers on television in the den. My grandmother, three aunts, and mom were in the kitchen kibitzing and preparing what can only be described as a feast for our large Italian family.

There were seven kids in that Pittsburgh basement – five girls and two boys, or so we thought. Six of us routinely played together while the seventh kept himself busy expertly building model cars with the most amazing precision and attention to detail. We played cards and board games. We played with dolls and stuffed animals. We hosted tea parties and we played dress up.

That was my favorite – playing dress up. We had this large container of old clothes, hats, and accessories that we would rummage through to find just the right outfit. In this, there were no rules. We didn't have boys' clothes and girls' clothes... just a treasure chest of fashion.

I recall adoring one article in particular. It was a floor-length silk skirt (at least it was on my five-year-old frame) with a beautiful organic pattern of earth tones that would make mid-century modern fans go wild. I loved everything about it. The way it looked, the way it felt and, most importantly, the way it made me feel. I picked it out so often that it eventually became "my skirt."

To a child, there wasn't anything wrong or weird about this. Nobody seemed to care which toys I played with or what I wore when we drank imaginary tea... so I didn't care either. I was doing what I wanted, what felt right. I was having fun and I wasn't hurting anyone. There was no fear, doubt, guilt, or shame... yet.

> *I was having fun and I wasn't hurting anyone.*

My grandparents were snowbirds, retired East Coasters who spent summers in Pittsburgh and drove cross-country to spend their winters in Tucson. After a particularly nasty divorce, my mom, sister, and I left Pittsburgh and moved to southern Arizona for a fresh start. Don't worry, you'll be happy to hear that my skirt came with us.

Shortly after our arrival, it was time for me to start first grade. Mom committed to seeking out the best possible education for me and my sister Gina. Incidentally, I couldn't say "Gina" when I was a baby so I lovingly called her Sissy. I still call her that to this day and, as you might expect, so does everyone else. And by everyone, I pretty much mean everyone including her husband, kids, and co-workers. Even Emily and Frankie refer to her as Aunt Sissy. We were enrolled in a parochial school affiliated with our Catholic upbringing. It was a beautiful campus with an impressive academic record. It was also one of the first places I felt alone, ashamed, and broken.

With parochial school came the requisite school uniforms, strict dress code, and grooming policies. The uniforms regulated most of what could be worn, but other policies limited everything from shoes, socks, and accessories to the length and style of hair.

These rules were unwelcome, strict, and largely gender-based. Boys had the option of wearing navy blue slacks or shorts with a short-sleeved white polo, ensuring that the bottom of the two buttons was always fastened and that the hair was no longer than the collar. Girls could wear a navy and gray plaid jumper or pleated navy shorts with a button-up white cotton short-sleeved blouse, ensuring that every button of the blouse was fastened except the top one.

> There was no fear, doubt, guilt, or shame... yet.

It's hard to imagine anyone desperately wanting to wear that hideous plaid jumper, but there I was, wishing I could.

This was the first time I was introduced to the idea that boys were not only expected to dress in a particular way, but that they were not allowed to wear certain clothes at all. In this oppressive environment, I realized that who I was, what I wanted, and what felt right to me didn't really matter that much, or at all. Gone were the days when it was okay to do what I wanted, what instinctively felt right to me, and what was fun as long as I wasn't hurting anyone.

In this moment, a war was waged between who I was and what the world expected me to be. I was intimidated and woefully unprepared for this glaring misalignment. Eager to please those I respected and depended on, I lacked the resources to defend my reality and fight for my identity. I joined the ranks of the opposition. I hid and denied significant parts of my identity and pretended that I was just like everyone else – holding my breath and protecting my shameful secret at all costs.

I desperately wished the people in my life could love me unconditionally, but with little evidence that was possible, I never gave them the chance.

Looking back on it now, that seems both unfair and unfortunate. The fear, guilt, and shame were simply too paralyzing. I surrendered, to avoid an uncertain outcome or, worse yet, rejection and pain. My environment, as well as the experiences and interactions I had at that impressionable age, made unapologetic authenticity inconceivable – but not impossible.

I rarely advocate for absolutes. I use the words *always* and *never* sparingly because they mean you must be absolutely certain a hypothesis is accurate one hundred percent of the time. In my experience that's exceedingly rare, so I tread lightly.

With that being said, I'm prepared to defiantly offer not one, not two, but three absolutes. You, me, and every person on this planet, without exception, are processing everything all the time. Look at all those absolutes – every person, everything, all the time. Despite my tendency to avoid absolutes, I use these without hesitation. You are subjected to a staggering number of inputs every moment of every day. Everywhere you go, everything you do, and everyone you meet gets to be processed so you can determine things like what you think of it, what to do with it, and how to react to it. If you noticed a pattern developing, you're right. It goes a little something like this:

If you think that sounds like a lot, you're right. Over the course of your lifetime, you're going to get plenty of practice making sense of the world around you.

Input

Ever feel like life is basically organized chaos? Me too. That's because it absolutely is. The world presents you with chaos and it's your responsibility to organize it.

Now more than ever, humans are subjected to an overwhelming amount of stimuli (input). Just think about all the personal interactions you have each day. From the moment you wake up, you engage with the people who live with you, be it family members or a roommate. Throughout the day, while going about your business, you have incidental contact with countless others. You communicate online or over the phone with friends, clients, and coworkers. You consume content through traditional media (TV, radio, websites, print) and on social media (Instagram, Facebook, TikTok, and so on). It's an all-out assault on your senses.

There are infinitely more stimuli than you could ever hope to process. How then can you moderate that input so you don't become completely overwhelmed and find yourself huddled in the fetal position, sucking your thumb and trying desperately to find your happy place?

Selective attention determines what you pay attention to versus what you ignore.

You learn how to not even notice some things while others command your focus and attention. This act of paying particular attention to one thing – while simultaneously ignoring something else – is known as *selective attention*.

What determines the things you pay attention to versus the ones you ignore? Is it coincidental or random?

It's not really either of those things. You may coincidentally pay attention to something specific, because it's loud or disruptive; however, in most cases, the distraction disappears from your focus as quickly as it appeared.

Selective attention is a process of filtering by relevance. When you (and by you, I mean your mind) determine that something is relevant, you notice and pay attention to it. Conversely, when you, and your mind, determine something is irrelevant, you handily ignore it.

Think of selective attention like a bouncer that you employ to ensure that only the relevant stimuli get admitted to the party. You know all too well that everyone is clamoring to get in. There simply isn't room for all of the stimuli, because you have limited space and resources and you certainly don't want to exceed capacity.

So, how does your "bouncer" decide what's allowed in? As you may have guessed, like any great party with expert crowd control, there's a "list." The bouncer works tirelessly to keep out the unwelcome "guests."

> *It's important to understand that ultimately you're still the boss. You're in charge, because the bouncer works for you, and you create the list.*

For simplicity's sake, the list is categorized into three types of stimuli:

- ❖ Stimuli that are routinely allowed into the party, because they are usually relevant to your life, and therefore easily make it past the velvet rope.

- ❖ Stimuli that are sometimes relevant, often involving something new, temporary, or situational. They're unfamiliar and therefore aren't on the list. The bouncer determines if they'll be admitted to the party.

- ❖ Stimuli that are never relevant to your life, that you are not interested in, and, worst of all, that you know are bad for you. The bouncer is on the lookout for these troublemakers and will deny them entry every time.

Keep in mind, the stimuli that didn't make the cut this time don't go away forever. They return time and time again, desperately hoping the bouncer will eventually let them in.

Conversely, just because something was allowed access today doesn't guarantee admittance forever. Selective attention is constantly adapting and evolving. The bouncer is always working the velvet rope.

Process

It's about time to get this party started. Now that your bouncer (selective attention) has expertly sorted all the stimuli clamoring to get in – by only admitting those that are relevant, important, and hopefully good for you – it's time to make sense of it all. This is when you step up as the host of this little shindig.

You have a few things to take care of before the party starts.

Processing the world around you is an intricate and delicate series of steps and stages, and they're all happening all the time.

Yeah, I said *all the time*. That's another absolute, and I still feel the same way about absolutes. When I consider the notion that you are always processing, I believe it's a certainty. What about when you sleep? Are you processing then? Yep. Your dreams – most of which you won't even remember – are your brain's effort to organize and process as you recharge. What if you're a yoga master and an expert at meditation and mindfulness practices who can achieve deep flow for hours at a time? You are absolutely still processing. In fact, this heightened state of focus, attention, and awareness may just be considered processing on a whole other level.

With proficiency comes efficiency.

The idea that you're processing all the time sounds positively exhausting, and it certainly can be. It can feel so exhausting that you might become overwhelmed and your whole system could come crashing down. Learning to manage this delicate balance is critical. You're the boss. You're in charge of the system and you monitor the process. As with most things, with proficiency comes efficiency.

Your ultimate goal is to acquire the tools necessary to develop a mastery of how you process.

Keep in mind that you don't fly into flying. First you crawl. Then you walk. And then you run ... so ultimately, you can fly.

The path to mastery is long. It starts with patience, develops with deliberate practice, and excels through deep understanding.

Output

At this point, the party is in full swing. You can finally relax and enjoy the fruits of your considerable labor. You're going to quickly learn that there are still a good number of choices available to you. Maybe you're ready for a beverage or snack. Maybe you want to have a quick chat with a friend at the party. Maybe it's time to let your hair down and show the world what you've got on the dance floor.

Whatever you decide to do and however you choose to act at the party represents your response to the input you've been receiving and the processing you've been doing.

You do get to choose, but that means not caring who's watching you or what they think.

As the host of your party, all eyes are on you. You're being watched and judged... for what you eat, your choice of drink, how you react if someone spills something on your new carpet, and maybe most of all, your dance moves.

It's hard to live in a fishbowl in which all your decisions and actions are on display for others to agree with, disagree with, and judge mercilessly. *Should I do this? Am I allowed to do that? Do they expect me to do something else entirely?*

There will be some who are okay with one thing but not okay with another. Then along comes someone who won't be okay with the first thing but totally excited about the second. Suddenly, the overwhelm sets in and you're paralyzed. You surrender what you want and need. You bend to the will of everyone else and abandon your duties. You are no longer the host. You are no longer in charge.

You find yourself going through the motions, unable to enjoy your own party. You no longer feel allowed to be who you are or to make choices for yourself.

Or so you think.

Turns out you are absolutely able to be yourself. You do get to choose. But that means being the first one on the dance floor, and not caring one little bit who's watching you or what they think of your sweet dance moves.

This is essentially the difference between authenticity and conformity. Being who you know yourself to be – proudly presenting that to the world and acting in alignment with the core of who you are – versus being who the outside world wants you to be – hiding and denying who you truly are and instead acting in alignment with what others expect from you.

Turns out you are absolutely able to be yourself.

You were first presented with these completely opposite ways to live your life at a very young age when it likely felt as though you didn't really have a choice. At that tender age you made the safe decision. You went along to get along, because the alternative was way too scary to even consider. And the consequences were too painful to bear.

Each time you made a choice to conform, it became easier. As it got easier, it became a habit. As you grew into adulthood, the alternative only got scarier and the consequences more painful.

I'm getting a little ahead of myself, though. First, it's critical that you understand the importance of all the factors and variables that contribute to you feeling forced into conformity in the first place, especially when authenticity was always within reach.

Environment

When you think about your childhood environment, what comes to mind? The street you lived on? The house you lived in? The school you attended? All the places you routinely played and who you interacted with?

What about the makeup of your family? Were your parents divorced? Were you raised by a grandparent? How many siblings did you have? Did you live in the heart of the city or out in the country?

All of these things, and countless more, make up the environment in which you were raised, and they all had a lasting impact on how you now perceive and process the world around you. They also influenced your tendency toward conformity or your commitment to authenticity.

One of the primary environments you learned from was your family home. The family in which I was raised was safe, loving, and *conventional*. I carefully chose that word because *conservative* tends to be politically charged. My immediate family – which consisted of my mom, sister, and maternal grandparents – was liberal but at the same time conventional.

Surrounded by fair and open-minded people who were accepting of those from every race, religion, and sexual orientation, I was taught to love and respect others. Equality was a right, not a privilege.

So, if my childhood environment and the people in my family were all loving, accepting, and respectful, why didn't I talk to anyone about how I felt? Why didn't I disclose my confusion and concern? Why didn't I ask for help with my feelings of dysphoria, shame, and doubt regarding my gender identity?

Looking back from a place of clarity and accountability, the short but not particularly sweet answer is: I chose not to. The more compassionate response – offered with tightly closed eyes, imagining myself in the Payless shoes of my younger self – is that even in this seemingly insulated environment, I didn't feel safe enough to reveal it to anyone.

I was a scared, confused little kid. My mom was just managing to keep it all together after a bitter and ugly divorce. Adding what felt like another burden to her overwhelm seemed unfair. Despite their openness, my mother and grandparents (and me, for that matter) were unfamiliar with the idea of gender identity, so acceptance and understanding of gender expression was limited. Like most of society at that time, they believed in the traditional gender binary. There were boys, there were girls, and that was all.

> *There was no one I could relate to or confide in.*

Even though I knew what I was feeling, I didn't know how to express it, or what it meant. It didn't help that I never saw anyone like me that was represented in a positive way. There was no one I could relate to or confide in.

Candidly, even if I'd had the language to communicate who I was and how I felt, I'm certain it would have been dismissed as a silly, immature phase. When I was young, it was fine to play with toys and games traditionally considered for girls. There was nothing emasculating about playing dress-up, having a tea party, or playing with Barbie dolls. Eventually though, there was a clear expectation that I would grow out of this behavior. A clear and distinct line existed between what boys and girls were expected to do and how they were allowed to express themselves. Boys have short hair, they don't paint their nails, they don't wear makeup, and they most certainly don't wear skirts or dresses.

It's worth noting that, to my family's credit, this somewhat narrow-minded, conventional expectation was mainly focused on gender expression. I was never shamed or judged for being emotional. Instead, I was encouraged to feel my feelings. Boys were absolutely allowed to cry. My quasi-feminist mother taught us that both men and women contributed to keeping the house, making the meals, and raising the children. There was no such thing as "women's work" and her place was not in the kitchen despite what my misogynistic and chauvinistic biological father believed and tried to teach me.

Influences

Humans have historically been social creatures that hunted, gathered, and relied on community for safety, support, and companionship. Members of today's human race may not be out picking berries or field dressing a wild animal for dinner, but they still value community and recognize the importance of a civilized society.

> *Today's human race may not be out field dressing a wild animal for dinner, but we still value community.*

Understandably, the more advanced the human race has become, so followed the complexity of its social structure. The rules, roles, and expectations of modern society can send you reeling. Where do you belong? How do you gain approval? Who will accept you as you make your way out of the nest and learn to fly?

Like many, my childhood and adolescent years felt less like learning to fly and more like learning how to fall out of the nest and plummet toward a hard and unforgiving ground. Not for lack of intention or effort. I was flapping my wings feverishly and had my sights set on the horizon; I just couldn't catch air.

Society's appreciation and understanding of the concept of an individual's gender identity (apart from the long-accepted binary) existed on a spectrum between harmful and total joke. Dangerous or laughable, threat or punchline. The best I could hope for was the apathy of the ignorant or complacent people in the middle. They were less threatening, but far from comforting.

I desperately sought representation. There were a fair number of pop-culture icons in the 1980s and '90s who had a unique way of expressing their gender. These people were the coolest of the cool and the bravest of the brave – rock gods and mega movie stars. I'm a proud GenXer, so I watched MTV and saw Prince, Boy George, David Bowie, Annie Lennox, and others bend gender in the most beautiful ways. Or at least that's how I see it now.

They were able to capture my attention and could have been positive and affirming to me. Unfortunately, because of my home environment, I outwardly judged and rejected them, all the while being exceedingly jealous of their identity and authenticity. In an effort to fit in with those closest to me, I feigned exasperation, pretending like I thought they were weird.

Pop icons like Prince, Boy George, David Bowie, and Annie Lennox were able to bend gender in the most beautiful ways.

These celebrities were so audaciously different. I was convinced they were attention-seeking showoffs. I couldn't imagine why anyone would act like that, dress like that, be like that. It was all for show. It was all an act. But I absolutely wanted to act like that, dress like that, be like that. Be like me. Be different. Despite that truth, I resented them for their shameless authenticity. How dare they be so publicly unapologetic when I didn't even have the courage and conviction to acknowledge who I was to myself?

Other than these beautiful and daring, yet unrelatable and deeply resented icons, I was left with the opposite ends of society's appreciation of gender identity and expression. Representation mirrored the social construct, so it too existed somewhere between deviant and total joke, dangerous and laughable, threat and punchline.

On the total joke end, I found the movie *Tootsie*, the television show *Bosom Buddies*, and the SNL skit *It's Pat*. And, how could I forget, Frank N. Furter the self-proclaimed "sweet transvestite from transsexual Transylvania" from the cult classic movie *The Rocky Horror Picture Show*.

Now, I will be the first to admit that comedy, when created responsibly, can cut pretty close to the bone without damaging the focus of the humor; however, when it's the only representation of a marginalized group, the potential for fallout is magnified. I saw some of myself in these characters, and that only added to my fear and confusion. I didn't know a whole lot about who I was or what I wanted, but I knew I didn't want to be laughed at.

> *I didn't know who I was or what I wanted, but I knew I didn't want to be laughed at.*

One particularly unsettling representation from the dangerous end of the spectrum was the serial killer Buffalo Bill, the lead character in the terrifying horror film adaptation of Thomas Harris's novel *Silence of the Lambs*. As the manhunt continues and the young FBI agent begins to profile him, there's a loose correlation drawn between the depraved actions of a serial killer and his struggle with gender dysphoria. Admittedly, the creators attempted to disentangle the two with dialogue that indicated the character was not a "diagnosed transsexual" (their word, not mine); however, by that point, the shocking visuals already ensured that an unsettling connection would be made by most if not all of the people in the audience.

Once again, I didn't really know a whole lot about who I was or what I wanted, but I knew I didn't want anyone to be afraid of me.

From the moment you're born, during your childhood, into adolescence and throughout your adult life, other people will have a considerable influence on you and contribute to how you approach the choice between authenticity and conformity. Who you spend time with, the places you go (or don't go) and the things you're exposed to all shape how you see yourself and how you see the world.

During childhood, you learned how to navigate this process and develop your worldview. Beliefs and morals were still being formulated. You were hopelessly dependent on your parents and other adults to help you mature and develop the skills to adequately protect yourself. Unfortunately, not all adults acknowledge this responsibility. They may not offer acceptance of who you are and they may not see the world as you do. Some adults are not all that invested in their children, nor are they committed to their healthy development and success. This creates another perfect breeding ground for conformity. This is a place where authenticity rarely exists and is unable to thrive.

> *During childhood, you were hopelessly dependent on your parents and other adults.*

My mother and grandparents were totally committed to my happiness and success, but they were unaware of what was going on inside me. Although gender issues were being studied and explored in the medical community – and fought for in the streets by the LGBTQIA2S+ community – most of society was ignorant as to what it meant to be transgender, nonbinary, or gender nonconforming. What's more, I was unwilling, or more accurately, unable to share the specifics of my experience with them. While they continued to protect my surroundings and help me develop, their worldview was unsurprisingly narrow. I am grateful for all their efforts, and I acknowledge that with my not being completely honest with them, they were doing the best they could with what they knew.

Experiences

Throughout your life you're going to have experiences that evoke a wide range of emotions. They will vary in intensity and duration and can encompass everything from small happenings to huge events. As a child you were largely at the mercy of your parents and other adults, but as you grow older, you gain some control over your experiences. Life has a funny way of reminding us, however, that we are always at the mercy of pressure, circumstance, and fate.

Although I was assigned male at birth and everyone called me a boy, things that were traditionally associated with the female gender were irresistible to me. They just felt right. To be clear, that didn't mean that the stuff traditionally associated with the male gender was repulsive to me. Not at all. They both fit. It all felt right. What didn't feel right was the traditional either/or binary construct of gender. There was no line between the genders inside me.

> *I didn't talk to anyone about who I was or how I felt.*

I didn't talk to anyone about who I was or how I felt – and wouldn't for forty years because I was convinced that it was wrong, and unacceptable. My environment, influences, and experiences instilled in me the idea that biologically you were only able to be either *girl* or *boy*. Socially, being girl or boy dictated what a person was allowed to be, do, and have.

In my conventional home, ambitious expressions of creativity and gender exploration were simply not allowed or appreciated. I outwardly agreed with my constructed worldview, but on the inside I envied those gender-bending artists for their talent and courage.

Once again, in fairness to my mom, there were a number of adolescent relatives in our extended family who could have won a gold medal in dramatic alterations to their appearance. They engaged in dangerous behavior and experimented with drug use. I'm confident that she associated an appreciation of those pop-culture icons with what she saw as a slippery slope from creative expression to dangerous behavior. I accept that my mom and grandparents were just doing what they thought they needed to do to protect me.

Learn

Your environment, influences, and experiences all contribute to what you learn and how you learn it. The way different people learn is remarkably similar. You first learn by watching. The environment around you, the people who influence you, and the experiences you have will all teach you something, directly or indirectly.

You may be attentively and intentionally observing someone. They may be trying to teach you something like how to play the piano, read a book, or even brush your teeth. You learn a lot of practical things in this way. You also learn a great many intangible – yet essential – things indirectly. You witness other people's words and behavior while in your presence.

Emily and I have a creative and intelligent child in the second grade. Last year, Frankie graduated from board books to chapter books, so she and I sit down frequently and read together. As you can imagine, with any new adventure, there are challenges that she gets to overcome. Chapter books introduced her to a great many characters and advanced elements like plot and theme. She also struggled with compound words and longer sentences. As she read, she asked questions and I provided her with instruction so that she could continue to read better each day. During these sessions, I was teaching and she was learning – directly.

Frankie frequently learns indirectly from our reading together as well. There are lessons to be had based on where we read, who's around, and what happens during the time we're reading. As a new reader, she sometimes gets frustrated. I remind her that learning something new tends to be difficult... and rewarding. I reassure her that it's perfectly natural to get frustrated, and I encourage her to take a deep breath and try again.

She knows all the letters and their sounds, and she can do it. I believe in her, and more importantly, she gets to believe in herself. She's learning about the importance of patience and confidence, and she sees that no matter how many times she interrupts with a question or asks for help, I respond eagerly. So, in that way, she also learns about kindness.

Frankie and I often read outside on our little patio. My wife is the family gardener and has created the most precious little utopia in our modest backyard. Although I helped with the construction of the patio and pergola, she's the one who adds herbs, fruits, and vegetables that look, smell, and taste amazing. (Honestly, you would think she's growing loaves and fishes based on the volume of what she produces. For her next trick, I've encouraged her to turn water into wine.) Every time Frankie and I read on the patio, I mention how fortunate we are that Mommy once again committed countless hours doing something she loves so that we can have a beautiful garden in which to read. When Frankie thanks her mom, she learns about gratitude.

Recently, we added appreciation to the list of things that Frankie learns when we're out on the patio. Just last week, she stopped reading to mention how beautiful it was to listen to the birds chirping while she read. In that moment we talked about the importance of appreciating all the wonderful things about nature.

She's also learning how important reading is. We do this cute little thing where I say, "Reading is," and she says, "fundamental." At first, I'm pretty sure she didn't know what that meant. It was just a fun thing to do with Daddy. Now she understands that reading makes things possible for her that would otherwise be unachievable.

One Saturday afternoon I asked Frankie if she wanted to go to our local Half Price Books and pick out her first chapter book. She said, "Sure," with a little less enthusiasm than I would have liked, but off we went. I would soon learn that Frankie, like most children, was learning indirectly pretty much every moment of every day.

On the way to the bookstore, I encouraged her to pick out a book in a series. Not knowing what a series was, I explained to her that it was a number of books with common characters and thematic elements that she could get invested in and read over time. She seemed more excited about that notion so I was encouraged.

At the store, she scoured the shelves looking for just the right series and found one that she had seen at school before – The Magic Treehouse books. After sorting through what seemed to be an endless stack of books, she picked one about dinosaurs.

Happy with her choice, we headed to the counter to check out. Frankie brought her little satchel with money from her piggy bank – because she was learning about what things cost and the value of money. She was also learning about how to save by buying second-hand books, and that doing so was both affordable and sustainable.

Up to this point we had only frequented the library, which is clearly the most economical and sustainable method, but this way we were able to teach her about being an intelligent and intentional consumer.

We arrived at the end of the line at nearly the same time as another customer. I invited that person to go first since it was the kind and polite thing to do. They graciously accepted with a smile and a thank you.

Ever the logical creature, and in an effort to decode what had just happened, Frankie mentioned that she thought we had gotten there first. I told her that it didn't matter who got there first, letting the other person go first was the polite, kind thing to do. She just smiled.

Before we were called up to the counter to pay, Frankie got distracted by all the shiny impulse-buy *tchotchkes* strategically placed at eye level. When the cash register attendant greeted us, I smiled at her and returned her greeting. Frankie was lost in a land of keychains, bookmarks, and tiny electronic fart machines. As I stared at my daughter and cleared my throat, she looked back quizzically, although I'm confident she knew exactly what I wanted. She then turned her attention to the cashier and said, "Hello."

Frankie and I have talked quite a bit about the importance of connection. She knows that connecting with others by looking them in the eye and using their name is a way of showing them you see them, you appreciate them, and that they matter to you.

She looked over at me and said that she couldn't see the cashier's nametag. I beamed with pride and told her that was okay. "Just ask her name."

When Frankie did this, the cashier looked equal parts excited that a customer took an interest in who she was and shocked that it was a seven year old.

The cashier's name was Jasmine. Her glasses were a fashionable statement piece as much as a tool to help her see. Her hair was a vibrant mix of colors and she was sporting a rainbow lanyard with various articles of flair pinned to it, including pronoun pins and other expressions of pride. I appreciated everything about her vibe and told her so with a special emphasis on my appreciation of her lanyard.

She lifted it up and looked it over as she thanked me and said, "Yeah, well you know, we've gotta represent."

I confirmed that we did in fact get to represent, and then my precious daughter offered, "My daddy's special too, because he's a *they*."

> "My daddy's special too, because he's a they."

I smiled at Frankie and Jasmine, realizing just how much my daughter was indirectly learning from me every minute of every day of my unapologetically authentic life.

These are just a few examples of how indirect learning takes place. The moral of the story is that people – especially kids – are always paying attention, and the quantity of indirect lessons is often considerably greater than those they learn directly.

Know

Everything that you're taught or have learned throughout your life can be described as "what you know." Some consider knowledge to be a relatively simple and binary concept. They figure you either know something or you don't. You've learned it or you haven't. Someone has taught it to you or they didn't. Seems simple enough, right? Well, not necessarily. Knowledge is intricate, complicated, and anything but binary.

I'm reminded of a quote from Albert Einstein, "If you can't explain it simply, you don't understand it well enough." That's a bold, albeit judgy, challenge from a brilliant man. Fortunately, he also suggested, "Everything should be made as simple as possible, but not simpler." Einstein was not a psychologist, nor did he study identity, human development, or behavior, yet in these two profound statements, he created the sweet spot where beautifully simple and elegantly complex intersect.

Like so many things in our intricate and complex world, knowledge exists on a spectrum. There are varying levels of knowing. Knowledge isn't fixed or static; it's ever-changing and growing. Knowledge is fluid.

I understand that you may want to keep things easy, given the complexities of life, but the consequences of underestimating the intricacies of knowledge are considerable and overwhelmingly negative. Uncle Ben taught Peter Parker that "With great power comes great responsibility." As Spiderman, Peter understood how to harness his superpowers and balance them with his responsibilities to create a positive impact on the world around him and the people in it. Seeing as how knowledge may well be the greatest power of all, I think it's time you realize you can do the same.

The most common way knowledge is oversimplified is to believe that once you learn something, you can check it off your list as something you know forever. You won't need to spend any more time or energy thinking about, worrying about, or learning about it. You are a self-proclaimed expert on that thing and that is all there is to it. But the world and knowledge are not that simple. They are ever-evolving, ever-changing, and ever-growing.

In 380 BC, an astronomer named Eudoxus created the first model of a geocentric universe, meaning the Earth was at its center. Eudoxus depicted a series of cosmic spheres containing the stars, the sun, and the moon, all built around the Earth. It wasn't until 1543 AD, when Italian scientist Copernicus wrote *De revolutionibus orbium coelestium* (*On the Revolutions of the Heavenly Spheres*), that he posited a theory in which the Earth and the other planets instead revolved around the sun. Despite being right about our universe, Copernicus was ridiculed and condemned for his heliocentric model. That's nearly 2,000 years of the greatest scientific minds thinking they knew something about the universe only to learn that they were incorrect.

This pattern plays out time and again in the scientific community. Take for instance the idea of the atom and atomic theory. The first mention of the atom as the building block of matter was around 400 BC by the Greek philosopher Democritus – you know, back when we thought the Earth was the center of the universe. Scientists and philosophers continued to consider, study, and discuss atomic theory for centuries. The one thing they knew was that the atom was the smallest form of matter… until the late 19th century when scientist J. J. Thomson discovered the electron.

Turns out atoms consist of even smaller particles. Who would have guessed? Scientists, that's who. They're curious. They employ the Scientific Method and relentlessly question, formulate, and test their hypotheses until they come to an indisputable conclusion. Then they test some more, all the while consistently seeking out new and different information, variables, and evidence, with the understanding that at any moment their hypothesis could be proven wrong.

Nobody necessarily wants to be proven wrong, yet scientists welcome the challenge and keep an open mind to the possibility, all in the name of scientific truth. What would the world look like if more people opened their minds to all the possibilities? What if more people were willing to learn beyond what they already know? What if people could acknowledge that they just might be wrong?

I'm not exactly sure what it would look like, but I bet it would be beautiful.

Believe

What you believe is similar to what you know, but these two things are not the same. Knowledge originates and is kept in your head, while belief originates and is held in your heart. Knowledge is a thought; belief is a feeling.

Like knowledge, belief is not binary. It exists in varying degrees and can change over time. But unlike the scientific method, which observes and tests, belief is essentially a choice. It requires absolutely zero empirical proof on the part of the believer. If a belief is called into question, it's answered with a show of faith. No one is compelled to show proof in defense of their beliefs. They just believe. The same is true of nonbelievers. These people simply do not believe. Common examples of belief and nonbelief revolve around religion and spirituality. Each person can believe or not believe in a higher power based solely on choice.

People describe their core values as "deeply held beliefs." The emotional attachment to these beliefs is undeniable and ensures that the devotion is considerable. People are usually more committed to what they *believe* than what they *know*.

This is where it gets complicated. There is no guarantee that knowledge and belief will align. They can even be in direct conflict. If you accept that misalignment is possible, you'll be better prepared to handle the situation when it inevitably happens to you.

What happens when you learn something that contradicts one of your long-standing beliefs?

What do you do when you learn something that directly contradicts one of your long-standing beliefs? What if your core belief differs from one held by someone you deeply care about? And what happens when you discover that something you thought you *knew* was really something you *believed*?

For some, the answer is clear. If they think knowledge is fixed and binary, they will disregard any new information that comes their way, since they were likely not seeking it out in the first place. They will cleave to their beliefs no matter what. They are hopelessly committed and see everything and everyone else as a threat. Expanding on what they know and challenging what they believe is not an option.

Those who quest for knowledge and are open to new insights will instead consider and evaluate new information. What they learn may encourage them to challenge existing beliefs, and even cause them to abandon a belief they can no longer hold in their heart.

The process of finding the strength and courage to navigate what we know, and bridging the gap between knowledge and belief is challenging. It takes focus and dedication and begins with the willingness to have an open heart and open mind.

Your environment, influences, and experiences shape your worldview. I learned a considerable amount from the people in my life about what to expect from the world, and in turn, what was expected of me. I learned what was allowed and what wasn't. Ultimately, those rules formed the system I used to make my way from childhood to adolescence, and from adolescence to adulthood.

Every person's system – regardless of how different they are – originates out of necessity. In an effort to navigate the complexities of life, a system allows us to create order out of chaos in a hectic world. Systems are critically important, and somewhat ironically, they're a byproduct of living. I bet you never sat down with the intention of creating a system dedicated to processing your life, the people in it, and the world around you. You simply developed it in response to a need.

It's critical to consider how your systems were formed, what they consist of, and how they evolve over the course of a lifetime. You get to learn everything you can about your systems so you can understand how they operate and the impact they have on you and your life. You get to continually evaluate, challenge, and update your systems to ensure they remain in alignment with all that you learn, know, and believe. Your systems contribute substantially to the most central and personal part of who you are... your identity.

2
IDENTITY

> "I believe that each of us carries a bit of inner brightness,
> something entirely unique and individual.
> A flame that's worth protecting."
>
> —Michelle Obama

I was five years old when we left Pittsburgh. We loaded what little we had into a small wood-sided trailer. My mom, sister, grandparents, and I piled into Pappy's beloved 1977 Lincoln Town Car. I didn't yet know how a trailer hitch worked or that putting our worldly goods into the trailer meant we were taking them with us.

As we pulled out, I stood on the back seat to wave goodbye to the relatives we were leaving behind, only to see the trailer following along, keeping pace and taking all the same twists and turns. I looked at my mom wide-eyed and shouted, "The trailer's coming! The trailer's coming!" as I jumped up and down. I couldn't believe it. I had so many questions. How did the trailer know where to go? What if it got lost? What would happen to all our stuff?

Rather than get frustrated, and without regard for a rigid travel schedule, my grandfather found a safe place to pull over so we could get out of the car. He patiently showed me how the trailer connected to our vehicle. He pointed out the hitch on the car, the tongue on the trailer, and even where the wires connected so the lights on the back of the trailer told cars behind us when we were braking, turning, and changing lanes.

My mind was blown. I'm confident this was not the first time my grandfather had taken the time to thoughtfully teach me something, and I'm certain it wasn't the last. Unlike my biological father, my grandfather loved me enough to continually invest in me until he lost his battle to Lou Gehrig's disease when I was twenty-five. The glaring difference between these two men in my mother's life is why she made the courageous decision to file for divorce. She knew that the person she once loved was not a great man like her father. In fact, he wasn't even a decent man. With the love and support of her parents, we left my biological father behind in search of a better life and brighter future.

When we first arrived in Arizona, we lived with my grandparents for a short time while Mom got her feet under her and figured out what to do next. With their assistance, we moved into a modest ranch-style house. It wasn't as lavish as the house we left in Pennsylvania but we didn't care about that. We were together. It was home and that was all that mattered.

As a single parent with obligations, responsibilities, and bills to pay, Mom had no choice but to get a full-time job to make ends meet. She wore all the hats – Mom, Dad, chef, housekeeper, landscaper, and on and on. It wasn't unusual for her to get up at 4:00 AM so she could throw in a load of laundry, make breakfast, pack lunches, and get ready for work... all before we got out of bed. Looking back on it now, I likely didn't appreciate just how committed she was to creating a great life for me and Sissy.

The fact that our new house was literally just a few steps from the back gates of our elementary school was not an accident. Although Mom had a village to help her, she knew that being able to safely walk to and from school would be helpful and convenient. After all, it was the 1980s, with no home security system, smart locks, doorbell cameras, GPS tracking, or cell phones. We walked to school each morning and home again after dismissal.

GenX kids were the first to return to an empty house after school, largely responsible for themselves until a parent finished work and came home for the evening. As "latchkey kids," the first thing Sissy and I would do was lock the door behind us. Then one of us would immediately call our mother to let her know we were home safely. If Mom didn't get a call by a set time, she would activate the "phone tree."

In the absence of today's technology, she had a long list of numbers for people who could vouch for our whereabouts. She would start with the school. If they didn't know, it was on to our neighbors who were home during the day. Next, our friends' parents. If there were still no answers, she would move on to local relatives – grandparents, aunts, and uncles each got a call. She would make her way through the list. The further down the list she got, the more irritated she became.

The amount our mother worried was equal to her love for us.

The amount our mother worried was equal to her love for us. This was reflected in her tendency to jump to conclusions the moment we were late. Her rational brain rolled right past the idea of harmless delays or distractions. Oh no, we were clearly in mortal danger! Her imagination would convince her we had been snatched, that we were in an accident, or that we had been mauled by a hungry grizzly bear on the fifty-foot walk from the school yard to our front door.

As you can imagine, Gina and I were not often late and we never tried to pull a fast one. With no CallerID, our mother had neighborhood spies in place to verify we were where we said we were. Chief among them was Shirley across the street. She was retired and sympathetic to my mother's situation. She would sit on her porch and wait for us to walk by, ensuring we didn't try any funny business. As a child it felt overbearing, but as a parent I totally get it now.

Sissy and I spent every afternoon home together. Back then, we loved each other, but we didn't particularly like each other. Despite being only a year and a half apart (she's older), we didn't have all that much in common. Fortunately, our appreciation for one another grew as we got older. Our families are incredibly close now, and I am grateful for her. Much like Emily, her expression of unconditional love and acceptance helped me to eventually love and accept myself.

Back to that house on Scarlett Street where I spent much of my time alone with my thoughts and feelings. I'm not sure what happened to my childhood skirt, but I didn't have it anymore. I suspect it ended up in the donation pile along with the books and toys everyone thought I'd outgrown.

The skirt still fit me, literally and figuratively, but it turns out I wasn't allowed to have a skirt anymore. I was too old to be playing dress-up. I was too old to try on makeup and "pretend I was a girl." I didn't think that was what I was doing, but I didn't know for sure what was going on or what my feelings meant. Even if I could've figured some of it out, I wouldn't have had the courage to talk about it. I mean, if pretending to be a girl was against the rules, whatever was going on with me definitely was not okay.

> *If pretending to be a girl was against the rules, then whatever was going on with me definitely not okay.*

That didn't seem to matter to my head or my heart. The attachment I had to that satin skirt became apparent. I wasn't so much thinking about the actual skirt as I was remembering how I felt when I wore it. It felt good. It felt right. It felt affirming. Candidly, it was even more than all that. It was euphoric.

I wanted my skirt back. Since that wasn't an option, I found other ways to express myself in the safety and privacy of my room. Using my imagination, I would put a t-shirt on my head and pretend I had long flowing hair to be brushed and braided. I would put on ChapStick and pretend it was lip gloss. I even had a pair of stretchy shorts that I could tuck one leg into the other so when I pulled them on it felt as though I was wearing a skirt. I did all these things while I played, read, or did homework in my room in the hopes I would sense a hint of those affirming feelings that I missed so much.

By using my imagination, I was able to create what I would describe as contentment. It once again felt right to me. Unfortunately, the serenity quickly gave way to a host of negative and damaging emotions. I was confused as to why something that could make me feel whole and complete was something that I needed to hide. I was ashamed that I was routinely doing something that those I loved and respected felt was wrong. I was terrified that, despite saying and doing what I was told, someone would discover who I truly was and what I really wanted. I wanted to feel whole, complete, and content... but not as much as I craved acceptance and approval.

> *I wanted to feel whole, complete, and content... but not as much as I craved acceptance and approval.*

As an adolescent I continued to explore my identity and expression secretly. I also found clever ways to express my feminine self that were socially acceptable and would not put me at risk of having my secret exposed to the world.

I was a teenage boy with a skincare routine who always wore ChapStick – sometimes cherry with a subtle red tint. I had soft beautiful handwriting that people frequently complimented. I was often told that I "write like a girl," whatever that means. I wore clothes made from soft fabrics in bright colors and bold patterns. I had no problem wearing pink.

Unlike many guys, I loved to go shopping with my girlfriend. Other boys would be perched on chairs near the dressing room with a purse plopped on their laps, annoyed and resentful, while I happily fetched different sizes and talked about which colors complimented her skin tone.

I liked to have my nails done, and I wore jewelry. I wore cologne that was less oak and musk and more citrus and floral. I was emotional, empathetic, and compassionate. I was a great communicator and an even better listener. In the 1990s, I was actually ahead of the curve. I was "metro-sexual" before it was cool. *Queer Eye for the Straight Guy* had just arrived on the scene, trying to get straight dudes more in touch with their feminine side, long after I was already there. Some attributed all of this to being raised by a single mother and having a sister. While I loved, appreciated, and looked up to Mom and Gina, that wasn't what was at work inside me.

There was a distinct and uncomfortable difference between who I was, how I felt, and what the world expected from me. Misalignments, although manageable at first, usually progress into a cognitive dissonance that leads to an identity conflict that needs to be reconciled. In those early years, I couldn't fathom a world that would accept and embrace me, so I figured my only option was to change who I was and how I felt.

> *There was a distinct difference between who I was, how I felt, and what the world expected from me.*

I didn't know it at the time, but gender identity is not a choice. You can't just decide one day that you are going to pick an easier or more convenient gender identity. So, I couldn't be my authentic self and I couldn't just change who I was. That left me with exactly zero good options for a healthy, sustainable identity. But let's not forget, I was young and uninformed, so I chose the super-secret, unhealthy and unsustainable third option – hiding and denying my gender identity. I foolishly thought I could just keep my head down, ignore how I felt, and deal with it. I hoped it would lessen in time or, better yet, just eventually go away.

Boy, was I wrong. It never lessened, and it most certainly didn't go away.

For a while, denial alleviated the discomfort. Then, what I thought was a viable solution actually became worse than the problem I was trying to solve. I began to develop a host of negative and destructive emotions like resentment, frustration, anger, fear, guilt, and shame. The impact of these emotions became unbearable so, once again, something had to change.

Denial gave way to deception. I was forced to acknowledge the reality of my feelings. However, I didn't have to openly admit them. It would be my personal and private deep dark shameful secret. Being who the world wanted and needed me to be and keeping my secret a secret would become the core of my identity.

The Definition

Identity is like a ninja. It's everywhere and nowhere all at once. And it's rather tricky to define. I'm going to once again take Einstein's lead and share with you as simple a definition as I can (but no simpler). Once you understand how your identity is formed and how it develops, you'll be able to discover who you truly are and what you really want... for maybe the first time ever.

Identity is your blueprint for
personal development and social participation.

It impacts every aspect of your life –
how you see the world, how you are seen –

and it serves as the foundations and filters
for processing everything around you

Wait, I committed to giving you a simple definition, right? I know that at first read, this definition can feel overwhelming, but with just a little work, the simplicity will shine through. Let's break it down, much as I would when helping my daughter Frankie learn a new compound word.

> Identity is your blueprint for personal development and social participation.

Personal development is a lifelong process that begins the day you're born. From the moment you take your first breath, you start developing a sense of who you are, and eventually, who you'll become. In that stage, you're completely dependent on others to provide for you, and you quickly recognize who those people are, and develop a profound connection and appreciation for the role they play in your life.

All the people and interactions you have in these impressionable years contribute to your development. But these external elements are not the only things that contribute to who you are destined to become. There are also internal elements of identity. No amount of external influence or experience can take these away or change them. Nevertheless, when subjected to an onslaught of pressure, you may be coerced into suppressing, denying, or hiding these internal aspects of your identity.

External influences can impact and overpower your internal identity because there are certain things they provide that you need to survive. Before you find your voice, you might feel you have no choice. You are expected to learn, comply, and tow the party line of those entrusted with your care. Your existence becomes more about being who you are supposed to be, and less about becoming the best version of who you already are.

Social participation, on the other hand, starts a bit later. Anyone with kids will tell you that changing diapers requires the

IDENTITY

participation of both baby and caregiver, but there's nothing social about it.

Internal and external influences impact your demeanor and tendencies, your core values and goals, your confidence and courage (or, as is more often the case, the lack thereof). How you choose to socially participate is

> *Changing diapers requires the participation of both baby and caregiver, but there's nothing social about it.*

often governed as much by a lack of confidence and courage as it is by an abundance of shame and fear.

The decision to embrace authenticity comes at the expense of the approval, belonging, and acceptance you crave. In the early stages of development and social participation, tiny humans find themselves in the regrettable situation where individuality and community are often mutually exclusive. You can either be who you truly are, or you can be who others in your default community expect you to be. When being different isn't understood or accepted, it results in rejection. The prospect of going it alone is terrifying. The human race has relied on community for survival, so acting any other way is counterintuitive and terrifying.

As you age, you come to realize that if one set of people refuses to accept you for who you are, that doesn't mean that all hope is lost. You have the option and the ability to seek belonging and acceptance from a different community. Admittedly though, this is not the easiest path.

> Identity impacts how you see the world,
> and how you are seen.

As you continue the journey, you naturally increase your social participation and widen the range of your social circle. You visit new and different places, meet new and different people, and do new and different things. Each new acquaintance has an influence on you, and each interaction has the potential to impact your identity. The lens through which you view and process the world is constructed from both what's inside you as well as from these external interactions. In that way, it's ever evolving and ever expanding... if you let it. The way you perceive and process the world, and the people in it, is deeply personal and unique.

If you and a friend were standing next to each other when you met someone new, what you would notice and the opinions you might form would be different. Who you are and the experiences you've had substantially contribute to what you see – regardless of who the new person is or what their experiences have been. In other words, your identity not only impacts how you see the world, but also your perceptions and opinions of others. The reverse is true, too; other people's identities impact their perceptions and opinions of you.

Their identity shapes the lens through which they process the world around them. Unfortunately, this means that they apply their past to the people they meet today... and that can include when they meet you. They use the people they've met, the places they've already been, and the experiences they've had in the past as a way of figuring out where you belong. They're determining who you are and how to label you so they know what container to put you in. On the surface that seems relatively common and harmless. I can assure you that it is in fact common but it is most certainly not harmless. Ultimately, it's not their job to determine who you are, what to label you, or what container to put you in. It's up to you to tell the world those things.

As your identity develops and your social interactions increase, you will meet and engage with people who have had different experiences than you. Inevitably, that means you won't fit into some people's containers. They will not have prior experiences that allow them to see, respect, or understand you. They will be confused by you and intimidated by your identity. They won't know where you fit or what to do with you.

The part of you that confuses them could be a relatively small part of your identity, or it could be a core part of who you are. Either way, in their confusion and resistance, they close their eyes to who you really are, and instead imagine a more convenient version of you that fits into their existing labels and containers. That way, they won't have to challenge what they *know* and *believe* in order to figure out how to deal with you. Unfortunately, that means you're likely to get saddled with labels that don't represent you. Rather than challenge their system, they'll remain ignorant by refusing to learn about the real you.

> *In their confusion and resistance, they instead imagine a more convenient version of you.*

When engaging in social participation, people (including you and me) are extremely protective and proud of their systems. They took a really long time to create and each of us is confident that we have the best systems ever, that they work all the time, and that they will never fail us. That's what systems do, right? They create order out of chaos. They make complicated things simpler, and they make hard things easier. Sure, that part makes sense, but it's irresponsible to expect that any system can work forever without modification or expansion. Every system eventually needs to be updated and upgraded to accommodate new information, current advancements, or unexpected variables.

Most people don't like it when their system is questioned or challenged. Making updates requires a willingness to open their mind and heart to new things. It requires a willingness to learn and even accept that they may have been wrong about something. Updates to their system have the potential to create internal conflict and external strife. So, rather than challenge an existing system and do all that work, people frequently try to squeeze, stuff, and smash others into ill-fitting containers.

The more inconvenient someone is, and the more that challenges their comfort, the more likely they are to dig in their heels and resist growth and change. It doesn't have to be that way, though. Since coming out as nonbinary and openly expressing my authentic gender, I have had the pleasure of finally being seen, accepted, and respected, just as I am. But I have also experienced the disappointment of people clinging to their existing systems while trying to force me into a container in which I clearly do not fit. Their container may be ill-fitting because they're trying to categorize me in a way that vastly oversimplifies my identity. Or, worse yet, they are intentionally and maliciously miscategorizing and mislabeling me in an effort to brazenly show me just how committed they are to their rigid belief system. Regardless of the reason and intention, the impact is the same. I don't feel seen, accepted, welcome, or safe.

> *The more inconvenient someone is, and the more that challenges their comfort, the more likely they are to resist growth and change.*

Like most of the things I talk about, how I'm received by others isn't binary. There are countless degrees of how people respond to me. I find that curious people engage me with an open heart and an open mind, fully prepared to challenge their system. They are willing, if not eager, to see me. Conversely, I find the stubborn people already have their minds made up. Their hearts are hardened to the possibility that I could exist (despite the fact that I am standing right there in front of them). Not only are they unwilling to see me, but they are outraged that I would dare show up and audaciously challenge their worldview... and their carefully perfected systems.

People are relentlessly committed to what they know as a part of their systems. The core of what you learn, know, and believe has been passed down from generation to generation by those who care for and love you. They committed to sharing what they learned, what they believed, and what they knew. The closer you are to these people and the longer you've known them is directly correlated to how much you "learn" from them.

> *People are reluctant to admit what they don't know.*

Admittedly, what they teach you is largely based on what they were taught, with some personal knowledge and experience sprinkled in. So, in many cases, your systems will not adequately prepare you to see, respect, understand, and accept all the people you will eventually meet.

People are also reluctant to admit what they don't know. It's unreasonable and irresponsible to think that anyone could know everything, yet there are plenty who consistently pretend to know it all. You do not want to be one of them. I'm sure you have met and engaged with a know-it-all. They're extremely irritating and absolutely exhausting. Common synonyms for this personality type are "conceited," "egotist," and "braggart," which makes sense because anyone who believes they know it all must think an awful lot of themselves. They are also likely to believe they're never wrong.

Are you getting frustrated just thinking about it? Yeah, me too.

I highlight these human tendencies because I first noticed them in myself. I found they had an impact on my identity formation, my personal development, and my social interactions. Everyone has the potential to engage in these tendencies and that's okay. They're called *tendencies* because they're common. Every one of us is human, none of us is perfect, and each of us is a work in progress. Being keenly aware of your tendencies, and learning to avoid them, is a huge step toward taking charge of your own identity.

As you decide who you are and who you choose to become, you will also learn how to create safer spaces. Genuinely seeing people requires that you venture outside of yourself and your history. In addition to seeking a safe space for yourself, you get to commit to seeing others for who they truly are, not how you want them to be. This requires empathy and compassion. Even though your story may be different and you might share little in common, you can still appreciate, understand, and respect others.

When meeting new and different people, you get to replace judgment with curiosity. Once you master this ability, you will no longer need to fit people conveniently into containers. You will no longer feel anger, confusion, resentment, or frustration when others show up and shine bright. Suddenly there will be a place for them in your system because you'll be willing to make room for them just as they are. Rather than restricting others to your current limited understanding, you get to continue learning and growing – with and from each new and different person you meet.

Each time you're willing to challenge your systems, you develop something known as *psychological flexibility*. This skill comes easier for some than others. Not only do you need to be open-minded and open-hearted, you also need to fully accept and embrace that you might be wrong about something. If just the thought of being wrong makes you cringe, you're not alone. Most see it as a weakness and will fight to prove they're right. But being wrong doesn't make you weak. And blindly defending yourself and fighting for what you think is right doesn't make you strong. It makes you rigid. It makes you blind. It makes you ignorant.

> *Ignorance lives in the long shadow of resistance and rejection.*

"Ignorant," by the way, is not meant as an insult. Ignorance is simply the absence of thorough knowledge or ample experience on a particular subject. It cannot exist in the light of education and understanding. Ignorance lives in the long shadow of resistance and rejection. Like so many things, ignorance is a choice. It becomes willful when you choose not to learn and grow.

> Identity serves as the foundations and filters for processing everything around you

IDENTITY

The particulars of your environment and your specific influences and experiences create the foundations and filters for your identity. They impact how you react and respond to the people and events in your life. There are many high-level foundations and filters that contribute to your identity formation. Here's a small sampling of some common ones:

- Biology
- Gender identity
- Sexual orientation
- Political affiliation
- Heritage
- Culture
- Race
- Religion

This list is by no means exhaustive. It's merely an example to add clarity and get you thinking about your own list. Everyone is subjected to these factors, but to different degrees, based on their presence or absence.

Foundations are introduced during a particularly impressionable time in your development, before you have a voice and a choice. This lack of voice and choice isn't inherently negative though. Can you imagine the number of children who might willingly put themselves in harm's way just because they can't yet appreciate the consequences of impulsive choices? Kids all over the world would be anxiously looking for nondescript white panel vans offering free candy and puppies.

Unfortunately, when your lack of voice and choice relates to something you are, rather than something fleeting that you think or want, it absolutely becomes damaging. Differences of opinion are not the same as a disagreement regarding your reality and existence. It's painful when the foundation embedded in you contradicts your ability to safely be your authentic self.

Filters are first introduced as you mature. A child in a sheltered environment, not exposed to outside influences and experiences, will progress differently than a child who is routinely encouraged and exposed to diverse outside influences. Both may notice filters that could be used as a lens to adapt and evolve their worldview, but being sheltered has a way of delaying things, making adaptation and evolution less likely.

Eventually, your voice gets louder and your choices more determined as you emerge from those impressionable years and move into adolescence. The process of individuation is critically important to your development. You eventually reach an age at which you get to say what you think and make up your own mind.

For the first time, you get to choose. You are developing into an individual with authority and agency, in charge of your own thoughts and actions. It's an exciting and empowering time. It's also daunting and overwhelming. The idea that you are now accountable for your thoughts and responsible for your actions can feel downright terrifying. The dramatic irony is palpable and laughable. You finally have the freedom you've always wanted, but your anxiety has you paralyzed.

You assemble all the negative consequences that could potentially become a reality and just assume they're a certainty. You fear the outcome of your authentic choices so vividly, you opt for conformity. You decide that the *fallout* you'll experience if you choose authenticity is far too great.

In fairness and compassion, the enormous pressure you feel in that moment is unbearable. In choosing conformity, you found safety. Fortunately, as you will soon learn, you can and will find safety elsewhere.

3

THE FALLOUT

> "Please try to remember that what they believe,
> as well as what they do and cause you to endure,
> does not testify to your inferiority but to their inhumanity."
>
> —*James Baldwin*

As far as childhoods go, I had a pretty good one. Tumultuous but good. I was surrounded by people who loved and cared for me. As you likely recall, this includes my single mother, an older sister by 18 months, and my maternal grandparents – affectionately referred to as Pappy and Nunnie. My biological father was not among the people who loved and cared for me and Sissy. He wasn't around much, but I suppose it doesn't take all that long to know bad when you see it, when you experience it. He had so little positive impact on my upbringing that I struggle to even refer to him as my "father." To me, that term isn't a biological title; it's one that you earn. He was so woefully deficient that in my angsty teenage years I started to refer to him as my "sperm donor." Angst notwithstanding, I don't necessarily disagree with my teenage self.

After years of emotional abuse, infidelity, and countless other transgressions, my mom filed for divorce. My sperm donor used his considerable power and influence to strongarm her into making a choice that nobody should be forced to make. She could either sign away her rights to all the marital money, property, and other assets... or face a lengthy legal battle she was not necessarily mentally, emotionally, or financially prepared to fight.

Despite all that and knowing she was unlikely to give up, he applied pressure to the one button he knew would work. If she contested, he threatened to file for full custody of me and my sister. If you're thinking that was a hollow threat, you're underestimating his considerable power and influence.

Throughout their separation, he made some pretty appalling threats. To make sure we knew he was serious, he allowed our home to be foreclosed on, at which time we were evicted, only for his brother to buy the house so he could conveniently move back in. There was no question he was both willing and able to make good on all of his threats. It worked. He got what he wanted. My mom took me and my sister and left everything else she had worked to build. That man was incapable of caring about anything other than himself, his money, and his ego.

> *My mom took me and my sister and left everything else she had worked to build.*

In 1981, we left Pennsylvania and moved to Arizona with little more than the clothes on our backs and a few belongings that, incidentally, did not include any of our toys or games. When my mother asked about them, my sperm donor said he'd paid for them so she could buy her own if she wanted us to have any. Vicious.

My grandparents spent the oppressively hot Arizona summers in Pittsburgh, and the brutally cold Pennsylvania winters in Tucson. Having basically no money, and in need of refuge, my mom, sister, and I moved into their small single-wide trailer with them.

I was blissfully unaware of our reality. My mother and grandparents protected me and Gina from the harshness of it all. They knew we would learn the truth one day on our own.

Pappy and Nunnie provided the safety and stability we needed when our family had little else. To me, it was an adventure that started by piling into Pappy's Town Car. We drove across the country, stopping at points of interest and staying in hotels that had color TV, swimming pools, and restaurants.

The adventure didn't stop once we arrived in Tucson, either. It was like one long, amazing sleepover with all of my favorite people. That single-wide trailer was the birthplace of a special bond among the five of us.

Although I have no proof, other than being a student of human behavior, I swear my sperm donor only filed for shared custody because he knew it would hurt my mother and grandparents. Imagine putting your unaccompanied five- and seven-year-old children on a cross-country flight, only to be met by the person who had destroyed your world. Now imagine doing it in the early 1980s, with no cell phones or GPS tracking. The infrequent calls home that we were allowed to make during our visitations were intentionally kept short by a hateful little man – both in stature and morality. It was abject torture for everyone.

We were typically subjected to two court-mandated trips per year. Admittedly, these trips were not necessarily difficult because Sissy and I had to visit him, but rather because it meant time away from our new home and the people we loved. One visitation usually took place in summer and the other in winter. Winter trips were hard because we were forced to leave during the holiday season. Summer trips were challenging because we were away from our mother for quite a long time. However, since Nunnie and Pap were snowbirds, we sometimes got to see and spend time with them while they were in Pennsylvania during the summer.

You may be wondering why he would allow us to see my mother's parents during those summer visitations. I think he allowed it because he didn't really want us. He liked the freedom and independence that a child-free life afforded him. The only thing he wanted more than discomfort for my mother and her parents was a comfortable life for himself. I know this because the longer he continued the charade, the harder it was for him to keep it up.

The number of times he waived visitation rights increased. There always seemed to be a reason – too much going on, work was too busy, or he didn't have the money for plane tickets. Soon, we started to see his justifications for what they really were. Excuses. He didn't have the money for our plane tickets, but he picked us up in a new Cadillac. What hurt wasn't that we couldn't visit as often, but rather that he clearly didn't want us to.

> *Soon, we started to see his justifications for what they really were. Excuses.*

For a while we would still get telephone calls from him. I suspect his motivation was to get under my mother's skin.

He had nicknames for us. I was his "cowboy," and my sister was his "princess." I initially thought these were terms of endearment, but his true colors eventually showed through. He was playing the part of a doting father but he was doing it poorly. The calls coming in for the cowboy and princess became less frequent, but they never stopped. He always called on our birthdays and on Christmas. Until my eighth birthday.

I had not heard from my sperm donor since the previous Christmas, and my birthday is in July. That was just about as far from Christmas as you could get, and practically an eternity for an eight year old. When I picked up the receiver and heard him say, "Happy birthday, Cowboy," I was a mix of emotions, none of them particularly good. I was sad, disappointed, and a fair bit pissed off.

I listened to what he had to say, then replied, "Thank you." After that, I asked why he never called anymore. The reasons – I mean excuses – flowed like a river after a downpour. The tears soon followed. I knew the real reason he never called anymore. It was all a matter of want. He didn't want to call. He didn't want us to visit. He didn't want us at all.

In that moment I made a decision. If he didn't want us, then I didn't want him. I told him that if we weren't a priority and he didn't want to call more often, then he shouldn't bother calling at all. I'm sure that's not exactly how I said it at age eight, but I am certain that was the gist of it. I vividly recall that as he started to make more excuses and lecture me about respect, I said, "*Fuck you*," and hung up. That was the last call the cowboy ever got, and the last time I spoke to my sperm donor.

The princess continued to receive calls for a little while longer. They were likely fueled by his anger, resentment, and a narcissistic need to get under my skin, now that I had been recently added to the list of people who had defied him and wounded his fragile ego.

Eventually, the calls ceased altogether. I didn't know it at the time, but the biggest gift my biological father would give me was his absence from my life.

I've shared this story because it's important for you to understand that my relationship with the people in my family was forged in a crucible of adversity. When someone you love is removed – or removes themselves – from your life, it leaves a hole that you're desperate to fill. For some, filling that void is like pouring water into a hole dug in the dirt. The more you fill it, the more the water soaks into the ground, only to leave you feeling alone, tired, and emptier than before.

The biggest gift my biological father would give me was his absence from my life.

Fortunately for me, I was not left alone to fill that void. My mother, Sissy, Pappy, and Nunnie each poured in a considerable amount of themselves so I could once again work my way back to feeling complete. That's not to say there were no personal or emotional consequences, but they would have been more considerable, and possibly even more dire, had these loving humans not stepped up and stepped in for me.

So, which of these special people did I finally find the courage to be my authentic self with? Which of these people – who loved, supported, and encouraged me through thick and thin – did I come out to?

None of them.

How is that possible? What was I so afraid of? Why couldn't I share my secret with the most special people in my life? They had shown me and even proven to me that they were willing to love me no matter what.

The truth is, I wasn't afraid they would stop loving me. I was afraid that their love for me might change or be diminished. But that wasn't the main reason, nor was it the only thing that terrified me. I was convinced that the consequences of coming out would be catastrophic. I couldn't conceive of a future when I could be who I truly was or do what I really wanted. In my mind, there was no world where I could trust what felt right, and in which I would accept and embrace who I was. There was no future in which a spouse would love me because of who I am, rather than in spite of it.

All the fear, guilt, shame, and doubt didn't originate inside me, but that's where it existed now, cloaked in the darkness of conformity with my shameful secret. They were created by a judgmental society that didn't much like different and held no appreciation for authenticity. All I could see were negative, dire consequences for me, the people I loved, and pretty much anyone who had ever known me.

Yeah, I'm laying it on pretty thick, because that's how it felt. It was a never-ending assault. Countless times, I thought I could muster up the courage to overcome hurdles and break through the barriers, only to find new, different, more challenging catastrophic consequences lying in wait that shattered my confidence and kept me right where I was... isolated, alone, and desperately afraid.

Why couldn't I share my secret with the most special people in my life?

I was paralyzed by fear. I believed that if anyone discovered my dirty little secret, the world as I knew it would come to an abrupt and tragic end. Everything I cherished would perish, and everything I ever hoped to accomplish would be lost. I decided to do whatever it took to keep my secret and protect what I had and what I wanted. Or at least, what I thought I wanted.

The only way to keep a secret is to never tell anyone, ever. Nobody. Not even the people you are closest to and love the most.

For these reasons, and so many more, I lived in hiding for over four decades. I denied my own identity because of the catastrophic fallout I told myself I would experience if I shared who I really was with the world.

The first time I used the term "fallout" to describe all the things we fear about unapologetic authenticity was during a coaching session. The person I was supporting was being particularly hard on themselves, unfairly critical of their ability to overcome fear. I needed to help them understand that they were not alone, and that their decision to choose conformity was an exercise in self-preservation. By choosing conformity, they were hoping for safety. They were merely taking shelter from what they believed would be complete devastation – the equivalent of nuclear fallout that would destroy their environment and all those they loved most. They confined themselves to their fallout shelter to survive.

> *I was convinced that the consequences would be catastrophic.*

This analogy highlighted the extent of their fear. They were finally able to acknowledge and accept that they weren't being a *chicken* (their words, not mine), but were instead terrified of "the fallout." They felt their only real option was to seek shelter. One of the gifts of this metaphor was a beautiful understanding, grace, and forgiveness that they were able to offer themself.

The idea of the fallout was familiar from my own journey. In that coaching session I gave a name and a face to a real but nebulous fear. For a long time, it felt like the villain from the classic 1980's movie *The Never Ending Story*. "The Nothing" worked its way across the land consuming everything in its path. The more it consumed, the more hopeless and helpless the characters felt. It wasn't until they faced "The Nothing," identified it, and gave it a name, that they were able to defeat what was eventually revealed to be a metaphor for grief, depression, and desperation.

The fallout starts as a thought or feeling that develops inside you. It's rooted in negative expectation that hasn't even happened yet. The fallout is a manifestation of a cognitive and emotional "what if."

The fear starts off small but expands quickly – it multiplies exponentially. Suddenly one "what if" becomes two. Two turns into four. Four becomes sixteen. Before you know it, you can't even do the math. All the nasty little "what ifs" are a part of you now, and they're relentlessly nagging at you. Any hope you had to fight them off is short lived.

The "what ifs" continue to expand, multiply, and band together to create one giant perceived fallout that's so massive you give up, frustrated and exhausted.

Like "The Nothing," the fallout is so damn insidious and menacing. It can have a massive impact on your decisions and, as a result, the identity you form and the life you live. It represents all the ways you allow the external world to influence and control you. It turns out you may not even be afraid of the action as much as you are afraid of the reaction. Of course, you're not alone. Everyone fears adverse consequences. They frequently wonder what other people will think of them. *Will they disapprove? Is what I want "normal" or "weird"?*

Ultimately, you must decide that the only person's approval that matters is your own.

You do your best to choose things that ensure the approval of others. Even if that means hiding or denying what you truly want. Sometimes you go so far as to become something foreign to yourself, questing after things you never really wanted. Continuing to seek acceptance.

Why do you do that? Because you're hardwired to. Humans crave belonging, acceptance, and approval.

But who's approval do you seek? To what do you want to belong? And what are you willing to do to be accepted?

You don't need to seek anyone else's approval to be who you are or to want what you desire most. Those decisions are entirely internal. With that being said, you can certainly consider the thoughts and feelings of those you love and trust, but the locus of control remains in your own head and heart. Ultimately, the only person's approval that matters is your own.

Nobody else is allowed to tell you who you are, or what you want.

When you first look outside yourself for permission, believing that who you are is not allowed, or what you want is irrelevant, that's the moment when you feel you no longer have a choice. That's the start of you losing sight of and abandoning your true identity.

How then do you reclaim what you've lost? What's the first step on the excruciating journey back to you? It all begins by telling yourself the truth.

Bill Wilson, co-founder of Alcoholics Anonymous, once said, "All progress starts by telling the truth." I love this quote for its elegant simplicity. He doesn't mention alcohol or kicking a habit or being sober. His profound statement is bigger than that. Lying to ourselves and telling stories to make ourselves feel better, or to justify our actions, is something many of us have in common.

Addicts lie all the time. In fact, an alcoholic once told me that because they're an addict, they're also a liar. To them, the terms *addict* and *liar* were synonymous. An alcoholic might say they don't have a problem, that they can quit anytime, or that they don't really drink that much. The deeper they spiral into their addiction, the more frequent and harmful the lies become. An addict will say and do virtually anything to protect their dirty little secret.

That sounds painfully and soberingly familiar!

I was hopelessly addicted to inauthenticity. Self-deception was necessary for my survival. I lied to myself and the world for so long that it didn't even seem like I was lying anymore. It was a mind-fuck of epic proportions.

I'd created an expertly constructed facade with the sole purpose of hiding the real me from everyone I met. On the surface, I was confident and successful. On the inside, I was isolated and afraid. At first, I was afraid that someone, anyone, would discover the real me. That they would expose me for the dishonest, broken, damaged freak I was.

As my charade continued, the fear grew and compounded. I was both afraid I would be found out and terrified of losing everything and everyone I cherished – my spouse, my career, my friends... everything. It was inconceivable that anyone could possibly love the *real* me.

Why was this fear so all-encompassing? What was driving my increasing anxiety?

The reason that the thought of anyone loving me unconditionally was impossible eventually became glaringly obvious.

How could anyone else love me when I didn't even love myself?

> *It was inconceivable that anyone could possibly love the* real *me.*

It's a commonly held belief that an addict will eventually "hit rock bottom." It's a place so low, so desperate, and so hopeless there's nowhere left to go but up. I'm pretty sure the path to rock bottom is different for each addict, but the negative impact and sense of desperation is the same.

I gained an appreciation of rock bottom the moment I realized just how much I resented myself. I was so far from being able to love myself that I actually hated who I was. That was the internal impact of feeling hopelessly broken. I had been falling for a long time. There were countless sobering realizations along the way, but none strong enough to elicit the profound feeling that only rock bottom can.

What made this acknowledgment so different? What changed? Why was I suddenly compelled to seek out my authentic truth for the first time, ever? Well, it turns out that my watershed moment was in becoming a parent. My reason was not a *what* but a *who*. It was my daughter Frankie.

Early in our relationship, Emily and I chatted about all the things that new couples do. When the subject of kids came up, we were very much on the same page. We both could see having kids, but neither of us was compelled to be parents. Don't get me wrong, we wouldn't trade being Frankie's parents for the world but, at the time, we weren't in a hurry. We were focused on being a couple, traveling, building our business, and achieving financial stability – easier said than done for entrepreneurs.

Eventually, the idea of parenthood came up again. This time, both of us were more receptive to the idea. We had lengthy discussions about the impact and implications of having a child and, in the end, we decided to go for it. No more birth control for us. Well, kinda. No more birth control, except of course, when our clients were taking us to Mexico, Central America, and the Caribbean for projects.

Emily made it clear that she didn't want to miss out on those experiences, and I don't blame her one bit. We both worked incredibly hard over the years to build the business, and it was time to reap the benefits of all that effort. I wanted her to be there for those projects, too. Our personal and professional bond was strong and we both loved to work and play together. We were one hell of a couple and I was genuinely excited to see what kind of family we would create.

One day, Emily looked across the room at me with a coy smile and a glow. I immediately knew something was up. She was pretty sure we were pregnant. My mind and heart flooded with countless thoughts and emotions. My primary reaction was shock. We never considered ourselves the couple who was "trying." We just stopped trying *not* to get pregnant and figured we would let the universe decide. We left it up to fate, and the universe had now spoken; we were going to be parents.

It had been over two years since we "pulled the goalie," and so we figured it wasn't in the cards for us. We were clearly mistaken. My heart was overwhelmed by excitement, joy, gratitude, and love for Emily and our unborn child.

As my heart got more used to the idea of being a parent, my mind was focused on all the logical and practical things that expecting couples consider. I couldn't begin to tell you all the things I was thinking and feeling; however, I can tell you with absolute certainty that none of them had to do with my identity... *yet*.

The Fallout

Emily and I love to walk and talk. We have lived in the same home for the last sixteen years. In that time we've taken countless strolls through our neighborhood, for exercise, or to get fresh air in our lungs and sun on our faces. It's on these walks that we discussed all the things that come along with being a married couple and business partners. Soon we would also be discussing all the things that come along with being parents.

Over many miles and years, a remarkable number of topics have been discussed. Countless ideas were conceived and, in the case of our pregnancy, startling revelations were made. One of the first, and funniest didn't seem like a revelation at all. When Emily was six months pregnant and we rounded the bend toward the creek near our house, I stopped dead in my tracks. I looked at my very pregnant wife and said, "Holy smokes, we're going to have a kid." She rubbed her belly and sarcastically replied, "You're just figuring this out now?"

My thoughts turned to the realities of parenthood.

Up until that moment, all our discussions and attention had been on "having a baby" – designing and furnishing the nursery, building a crib, buying a metric ton of diapers. *Baby, baby, baby.* During this walk, my thoughts turned to the realities of parenthood. Sure, we were about to have a baby, but we would also one day have a toddler, a kid, a teen, and eventually an adult who we would get to love, cherish, and adore.

What's more, we were going to be responsible for this person. It would be our job to support, encourage, discipline, teach, and prepare our child for each milestone, preparing them to lead a productive and fulfilling life in which they would hopefully enrich the lives of others and have a positive impact on the world.

No pressure, right?

As Emily saw the panic wash over me (as it often does), she smiled empathetically and proceeded to reassure me. She told me that she knew all this already. Of course she did. If I didn't love her so much, her habits of being insightful, calming, and generally right most of the time would be annoying. She went on to say that having a relationship with our child as an adult, like the one she has with her mom, is one of the things she was most looking forward to as a parent.

See what I mean? Epic insight from my brilliant wife. I'm confident that a seed was planted inside me on that walk. A seed that would grow into a mighty oak that eventually cast a shadow of doubt on my manufactured identity and the future relationship I would have with my child.

Another walk-induced realization was going to do more than just water that newly planted seed in my subconscious. It was going to create the ideal environment and provide everything that was needed for the seed to grow fast and strong.

Emily and I were on the back half of our walk. We turned the corner and made our way up the street that was home to adorable mid-century homes nestled in the shade of old growth trees. We waved to a neighbor as he read the newspaper and smoked his morning cigar in a rocking chair on his porch. There was something comforting and nostalgic about knowing that so many of our neighbors had started their own families and raised their children here, just as we were about to do ourselves. This is where our child would grow up, play, and meet new friends on the playgrounds and parks. This is where we would trick-or-treat and drive around to take in all the holiday decorations, listening to Christmas music, eating a candy cane, and drinking hot chocolate all the way, filling us with the joy of the season and a sugar rush that meant staying up late watching our favorite holiday movies.

I got all that from waving at our neighbor? Clearly I was in emotional overdrive. Somehow, everything took on an increased level of importance based on the impending arrival of our child. Collectively, however, everything in our own lives became just a little less important.

THE FALLOUT

How is it possible that things can be both more important and less important at the same time?

> *Every item of discussion took on fresh importance based on the impending arrival of our child.*

The truth is, when you find out you're going to be a parent, there is an undeniable shift in your personal priorities. Something that you didn't know existed moments earlier, suddenly becomes the most precious and important thing in your life. Your child shoots to the top of this list faster than a Taylor Swift midnight release.

A shift and recalibration of your priorities happens concurrently. Things that used to be of considerable importance cease to really matter to you. Things you never considered at all, now demand your attention, and items that were previously irrelevant now demand your full focus. It's hard to make sense of it all.

Up is down, and down is up.

Cats are barking, and dogs meowing.

Welcome to parenthood!

Stay ready so you don't have to get ready, expect the unexpected, and may the odds be ever in your favor.

When I think about people hitting rock bottom, myself included, it seems like the impact would be sudden and violent. Have you ever had that dream where you're in a freefall, and you feel a euphoric sense of freedom... right up until you realize there is nothing to stop you from smashing against the unforgiving ground, at which point you wake up in a cold sweat?

Hitting rock bottom seems like it should be an unstoppable force meeting an immovable object. Maybe it is for some people, but that's not how it happened for me. It wasn't so much a freefall as it was a steady slide, like rolling down a hill into a pit of sadness, anxiety, and despair... steady rather than rapid, almost hard to notice.

I did recognize that something was happening, but the realization was more confusing than frightening. The slow and steady nature of decline allowed me to largely ignore and disregard it. I was able to pretend that the fears didn't matter. I told myself that everything was just fine. I was an addict in denial, one who had deluded myself into believing that I didn't have a problem.

> *I was an addict in denial, one who had deluded myself into believing that I didn't have a problem.*

Eventually, I found myself at rock bottom just the same, and once there, nothing much changed. There was no sudden or violent impact that could wake me from my nightmare in a cold sweat. I quietly settled in and accepted my fate. I confined myself to a hole so deep, so dark, it was devoid of light and hope. The only thing I had with me was the last thing I needed – a shovel.

This analogy is drenched in Alanis Morrisette vibes. *Isn't it ironic, don't you think? Yeah, I really do think!* In a tragic twist, I dug the hole in which I was now confined. Admittedly, the outside world broke ground and handed me the shovel, but it was me who continued to dig and dig.

A common misconception is that rock bottom is always an immediate catalyst for change. Nope. As a functioning addict of inauthenticity, I was an expert at keeping the status quo. I'd learned how to compartmentalize like it was an Olympic sport. I was out to win the gold. In fact, I was the Michael Phelps of compartmentalizing. So much so that my friends would jokingly ask if they were going to get "business Don" or "relaxed Don" today.

I learned how to be what the world needed me to be, how to do what was expected of me, and how to hide all those things I wasn't allowed to be and do. This was my fate. So be it. I was the only one confined to my hole, the only one suffering – or so I thought.

The idea that my loved ones were not suffering because of my relentless commitment to an inauthentic life was another ridiculous lie I told myself. Looking back on it now, I understand there was considerable fallout from *not* coming out.

> *I was the only one confined to my hole, the only one suffering – or so I thought.*

Lub-dub, lub-dub, lub-dub. I held Emily's hand, listening to Frankie's rapid heartbeat for the first time. It was the sweetest, most precious sound we'd ever heard. That sound and those tears made our pregnancy really real.

At that moment, I began to learn remarkable things about love, with Frankie as my teacher. I didn't know that love could be both instantaneous and immeasurable, but that is exactly how I felt when I heard that tiny little heartbeat. I was prepared to spend the rest of my life committed to showing her that my love for her was unconditional and immeasurable, every single day.

That's when the panic set in. I could no longer deny the reality of my situation – hiding who I was, and denying what felt right was suddenly bigger than me.

Emily doesn't complain much. She is one of those optimistic people who deals with whatever life throws at her without so much as a peep. She deftly dealt with the inconveniences and discomforts of pregnancy. So, when she suddenly started to suffer from migraines she described as agonizing and intolerable, I knew it was serious.

Despite all the tests the doctor performed, he couldn't determine the cause. With just two weeks until the due date, he decided there was no reason for Emily to suffer further or risk other serious complications. We were scheduled to be induced that weekend, so we did what any young couple about to welcome a baby into their family would do… we enjoyed a lovely dinner out and saw a movie before checking into the hospital on an unseasonably warm Saturday evening in October.

Along with her optimistic personality, my wife has a near superhuman tolerance for pain. Because of the way her body reacted to the medications used to induce her, Emily's labor was extra long and challenging. It lasted over twenty-four hours with contractions largely at the peak of discomfort. It was both remarkable and humbling to witness.

Frankie was born at nearly eight in the evening on a Sunday night. That exact moment is equal parts a blur and razor sharp. A million thoughts ran through my head, and I was completely overwhelmed by emotions. I was also sleep deprived. I cried immediately, which won't come as a shock to anyone who knows me.

While they did the whole newborn version of the NASCAR pit crew thing, I gently embraced Emily, kissed her, and told her how much I loved her. When they were finished assessing Frankie, they put a bonnet on her head and placed her on Emily's bare chest and covered her with a blanket.

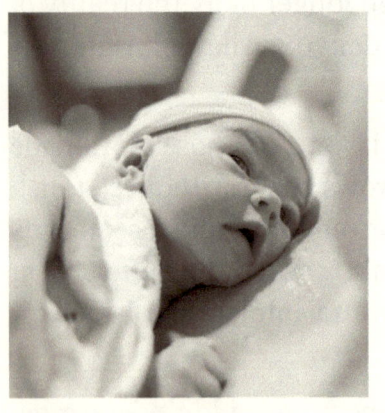

The sight of my child resting on Emily took my breath away. It was as if each new moment of the experience was better and more powerfully emotional than the last.

Next up was holding Frankie in my arms for the first time. It's difficult to describe how special that moment was. I was full of love, joy, and every other positive emotion… all the ones that are frequently elusive and in short supply. I felt completely content. I wanted it to last forever. I knew that it wouldn't, or maybe more accurately, it couldn't.

One of the first things Emily and I learned as new parents was how important it is to sleep when the baby sleeps. You can hope and pray that your efforts to get the infant into a routine and onto a schedule will be successful, but in all reality there are days when children are going to do what they want, when they want, and that defiance includes sleep.

Most days were pretty predictable. This particular day was not. Frankie had not slept well overnight. She got up early, was fussy, and refused to sleep most of the day. She finally fell asleep in the afternoon so Emily and I laid down to take a nap. It may have been the best nap ever. Frankie slept for hours and we did the same.

She woke in the early evening, just long enough for us to dote over her and feed her. Despite the long nap, she fell asleep again on Emily's chest. It wasn't uncommon for her to fall asleep while nursing. To me that was a beautiful expression of how comfortable she was and how safe Frankie felt there with her mother. I had a lot to learn from my beautiful daughter.

After we savored this moment, Emily motioned for me to come get Frankie, so I scooped her up and placed our daughter gently in her crib. Emily waited for me by the door. I slowly and quietly made my way across the room, trying not to reawaken the Kraken. Before we exited, I gently pulled Emily in for a hug where I could have remained for a lifetime.

After closing the door and swinging by our room to pick up the baby monitor, we were fairly certain that we had a little time to spend together. Having just had a lovely and refreshing nap, we were uncharacteristically awake. We decided it was a good night for a movie so we assembled popcorn, snacks, and drinks and settled in to pick the evening's entertainment.

Gone were the days of limited selections at a local video store. I vividly recall Friday nights at Blockbuster, hoping to stock up for a weekend's worth of movies, only to find rows and rows of empty boxes representing the hottest new releases you wouldn't be watching that weekend. If I was particularly desperate, I would politely ask the blue polo-clad attendant to check the return box. At that point, it was a coin flip as to whether I would leave the store having won the video rental lottery or if I would have to settle for something less than the hot new release.

Netflix soon became the gold standard around this time, offering streaming services in addition to mail-order DVD delivery. Streaming presented quite the opposite challenge to the rental store – a virtually unlimited catalog of movies available 24/7/365, and getting larger every day. In a lot of ways, picking a movie went from disappointing to daunting.

As Emily and I scrolled the cover images of countless movies, the all-seeing, all-knowing algorithm recommended rom-coms for me and action flicks for Emily, in equal measure. The cover art for one immediately piqued my interest. I didn't know anything about the movie but I was struck by the image.

> *I didn't know anything about the movie, but I was struck by the image.*

The film was *The Danish Girl*. Not exactly a rom-com but certainly not the action or sci-fi epic that Emily tends to prefer. I asked her what she thought and she said it looked interesting.

In the event you haven't seen the movie or read the book, *The Danish Girl* is based loosely on the lives of Danish artists Lili Elbe and Gerda Wegener. The movie stars Eddie Redmayne and Alicia Vikander and was released in 2015. Lili was born Einar Wegener and was among the first known transgender women in recorded history.

Early in the movie, I immediately connected with and could relate to Einar and Gerda. They were a couple, they were creatives, and they were very much in love, just like Emily and me. When Gerda's portrait ballerina model canceled at the last minute, she asked Einar to sit in so she could work on her painting. He lovingly agreed.

She asked him to pull on tights and wear her ballet slippers. He also put a beautiful gown over his clothes and she applied a hint of lipstick.

As Gerda painted, it became clear that what started as a reluctant chore for a dutiful husband became something more. Being in the gown and wearing lipstick stirred something inside Einar. The feeling of the fabric on his skin and the femininity was intoxicating. And, I suspect, terrifying. He found himself lost in the moment.

The arrival of the couple's friend startled Einar back to reality. The moment evaporated and his euphoria was replaced with shame and embarrassment.

> *...what started as a reluctant chore for a dutiful husband became something more.*

As one might expect in early 20th century Paris, Gerda was more curious than judgmental. She proceeded to celebrate the beauty of the moment. She kissed him on the cheek and named his feminine counterpart Lili.

There's so much beauty to be found in these moments of love and acceptance. Gerda then decided that she wanted to sketch her husband as Lili. Einar feigned reluctance while secretly reveling in the notion of experiencing the euphoria that he'd felt as Lili once again. They both had so much fun with the playful nature of this experience they took it a step further and dressed up and left the house as Gerda and Lili. What started as something fun and flirty for them both became something much greater for Einar. His experiences as Lili upended his world. Despite initial efforts to ignore how he felt, his true identity would not be denied. She was always Lili pretending to be Einar for the entirety of her life because she didn't know how to be anything else.

I sat next to Emily on our couch, completely transfixed as the story, my story, unfolded. Just like Einar, I lived in an invisible shelter designed for me by a judgmental society, built with bricks fashioned from my shame, guilt, and fear. It opened my heart and mind to a reality that I had long since accepted as impossible. It showed me what life might look like if I could only find the courage to fight the fear, confront the conflict between who I really am and who I allowed myself to be, and answer the question "What if I chose authenticity over conformity?"

There wasn't anything otherwise remarkable about our day, and I certainly hadn't expected our movie choice to serve as a life-changing catalyst. I didn't know it at the time, but this film would have an indelible and powerful impact on me. It encouraged me to later trust in Emily's love by vulnerably sharing with her the secret I'd been hiding, for the entirety of my life because I didn't know how to do anything else... *yet*.

Being a parent was about to kickstart something inside me that I never could have expected. I didn't want Frankie to get to know and grow to love the fragmented, manufactured version of who I was. Being a parent, her parent, would push me to do the one thing I long ago decided was impossible. I would find the courage to show the world exactly who I was. I would do it for her. I would do it for myself. And I would start with Emily.

4

LETTING SOMEONE IN

"If you possess enough courage to speak out what you are, you will find you are not alone."

—*Richard Wright*

Emily has those mysterious and beautiful eyes that change color based on what she's wearing, her environment and, I'm convinced, her mood. We met in the summer of 2006 in a dimly lit bar, late in the evening. She was rockin' a stunning green dress, a fierce red fauxhawk, and what felt like six-inch heels. Having just come from a fashion industry event, she was the epitome of style, class, and glamour. I was thunderstruck.

On one of our early dates, we took our cameras to the nature preserve, and it was there that I truly appreciated the depth and beauty of her eyes. They were vibrant and they were every shade of green you can imagine. If you've been to Ireland, you know what I'm talking about. When the clouds part on the often overcast, gloomy Emerald Isle and the bright midday sun shines down on the landscape, the countryside appears a transcendent display of green.

Emily and I were a team as we navigated the uncharted waters of parenthood. We had countless new responsibilities. In those first few days, our primary focus was keeping the new human safe and alive. Emily was a natural and it was a profound joy to witness her take to motherhood so quickly. I followed her lead and we found our rhythm. Don't get me wrong, there were times when we were confused, stressed, and tired. More accurately, the confusion and stress came and went, but the tired was always there.

Strangely enough, we may not have liked the stress, confusion, and exhaustion all that much, but we learned to love and appreciate them because they were a part of parenthood and therefore a part of the joy.

We were genuinely happy and content, as a couple, and as a family. Yet as an individual, my internal happiness and contentment would wax and wane. My temperament was delicate and my mood volatile. I couldn't predict when sadness and discontent would come, or for how long they would stay. They cast a shadow on my beautiful new life. At first, they were infrequent and short lived, but as time wore on, that shadow overstayed its welcome.

> *I could not predict when sadness and discontent would come, or for how long they would stay.*

There I was, going about my business, living my life, getting the hang of the whole parenting thing, and doing what I would consider to be a reasonably good job. Then, all of a sudden out of nowhere, I became consciously aware that something didn't feel right. I couldn't quite put my finger on it but something was off.

It started as an annoying, uneasy feeling. As a new parent, I figured it just came with the territory. Turned out I was wrong. That uneasy feeling inside me had nothing to do with parenthood; however, I would eventually learn that it had a lot to do with Frankie. Who we truly are, and who we allow ourselves to be, are not always the same. In fact, I'll go so far as to say they are rarely the same. Authenticity is hard. It requires strength, courage, and confidence. Most challenging of all, it requires a willingness to be vulnerable. It means making an unwavering commitment to be exactly who you are, everywhere you go, no matter who you're with. For the first four decades of my life I couldn't find that conviction. I was unwilling to be vulnerable. I was never able to make that unwavering commitment to myself. Until we had Frankie.

That relentless uneasy feeling inside me grew difficult to ignore. I found myself "on edge" and quick to frustration and anger. Despite being absolutely exhausted, I struggled to get restful sleep... which of course only made things worse.

I developed anxiety for the first time. I'd worked in some pretty stressful environments as a hospitality professional and entrepreneur. I'd routinely felt and managed stress but never felt physically anxious. I'd naively thought stress and anxiety were essentially the same. I quickly learned they were not.

For me, stress is more psychological. As soon as I started to feel anxiety, I knew it was too late to do anything about it. Everything felt heavy, as if I had weights attached to my wrists and ankles. There was a crushing load placed on my shoulders.

Every moment and every movement were exhausting. It took all my energy to perform the simplest physical actions. I could already feel my chest start to constrict. I couldn't breathe. Something had me in its grip, and it was squeezing the life out of me. I struggled to catch my breath like a fish out of water. I was flapping and flailing on the ground, desperate for water but helpless to find it.

> *Something had me in its grip, and it was squeezing the life out of me.*

Humans are largely conflict averse. Sure, you may occasionally meet someone who thrives on it, but for the most part, people are happy to avoid conflict whenever possible. Ironically, conflict is perfectly natural and frequently exactly what you need.

When you think of conflict, you likely envision a battle of wills between two different people. However, some of the most devastating conflicts happen internally.

The uneasy feeling inside me was a wake-up call that the epic battle between who I knew I was and who I allowed myself to be had begun. The sleeplessness, frustration, anger, and anxiety were escalations designed to make it harder for me to ignore the war that was raging. My refusal to admit what I knew to be true in both my heart and my head was the origin of it all. I was the one responsible for my inability to breathe. By finding the strength and courage to confront the conflict inside, I would finally be able to breathe again by sharing the thing with Emily that I had never told anyone in my then forty years on Earth.

> *Some of the most devastating conflicts happen internally.*

That morning, I'd picked up the phone to call her. I *needed* to talk to her, but she was spending time with her mom who was visiting from Colorado. As much as I did not want to be a bother or interrupt their time together, I recognized that *want* would not be strong enough to dispel the *need* I had in that moment.

I took a deep breath and dialed. I can't recall specifically how she answered the phone, but it doesn't matter. The sound of her voice hit me like a swift punch to the gut. I was physically nauseous. Those feelings of fear, guilt, and shame united to become a powerhouse of self-doubt. How could I do this to her? How could I put this on her? I always wanted to make her life simpler, not more complicated!

As I worked to gather my thoughts and emotions, we engaged in customary small talk. Our interactions are always so effortless and comfortable, and I didn't want to lose that. I didn't want to be the one to introduce angst and discomfort.

I could feel the strength of my resolve waning. I sensed that we were approaching one of those natural pauses in a conversation when a change in course and topic would seem natural. I closed my eyes and said to Emily that I had something I needed to talk with her about.

"Sure, go ahead"

—"No, in person!"

It resonated like an off note from an instrument tragically out of tune. It was neither effortless nor comfortable. Sure, for some couples this would be a perfectly natural exchange, but for us, the intentional effort to schedule a time to talk about something was anything but natural.

"Is everything okay?"

I fought back the tears.

—"It will be."

Admittedly, I was not certain that was true. But much like how fear, guilt, and shame became a powerhouse of self-doubt, the feelings of love, faith, and trust united to become a powerhouse of hope.

Emily asked if her mom would be willing to watch Frankie so we could have a chat. What grandmother would miss an opportunity to spend quality time with her ten-month-old granddaughter?

As we got ready to leave the house, I felt myself getting increasingly anxious. I was a bundle of mixed emotions. My head was foggy, which made it hard to concentrate. Keys? *Check.* Wallet? *Check.* Make sure Kathy has everything she needs to keep the baby alive? *Check.*

It was August in North Texas, so to say it was hot is a bit of an understatement. Leaving the comfortable confines of an air-conditioned home, car, or body of cool water was oppressive. With that in mind, you can imagine the look on Emily's face when she asked where we were going and I responded, "Let's just go to the park."

"Um, okay. Are you sure? It's pretty hot today."

This was Emily's tactful and delicate way of asking if I had completely lost my mind. Little did she know that both my mind and heart were at full capacity just focusing on getting through this conversation.

—"Yeah, it'll be okay."

This wasn't only my response to Emily's questions and concern about the heat. They were also the words I desperately needed to hear as we backed out of the driveway. I was trying to convince myself that it would in fact be okay.

There we were in the park, in August, in Texas. The heat was fitting, given the hell I had confined myself to.

Emily and I don't have secrets. It started with us as a couple, then as business partners, and now as parents. We've always been proud of that. I'm confident it seriously contributes to the ease and flow of our relationship. To acknowledge that I had kept this one thing about my identity from Emily for all these years was nothing short of heartbreaking. If given the chance, I would go back and do it differently. Of course, that would have required me to have been truly honest with myself first.

"Okay, what do you want to talk to me about?"

This is the part where I wished I had it all worked out in my head. I'd love to be able to say that I eloquently and succinctly shared my thoughts and feelings with Emily as we walked hand in hand through the park, enjoying the sights and sounds of nature around us.

Yeah, that didn't happen.

We found a small area with a pergola with shade that would offer much needed relief from the blazing hot sun. I sat on the top of the picnic table and put my feet on the bench below. Despite all the build-up and bluster, I had no earthly idea what I was going to say or how to express what I was feeling.

As I worked to gather my thoughts, sort my feelings, and consider which words to use, I could feel it rise up. Thought and logic were abruptly thrust into the back seat. My emotions took the wheel.

> *Despite all the build-up and bluster, I had no earthly idea what I was going to say.*

I opened my mouth hoping some words, any words, could fight their way forward. They could not. I had to settle for tears. I looked at Emily and I cried. Oh, how I cried. Earnestly, I'm not sure that does justice to my emotional outburst. I uncontrollably sobbed so hard and for so long I struggled to catch my breath. It was the physical culmination of decades of mental and emotional repression unleashed in that one moment and with that one person.

Emily pulled me close and held me tight as I completely let go and fell entirely into her loving embrace. The tears were an odd mixture of happy and sad. I was about to be free of a burden and weight that I'd resigned myself to carry for the entirety of my life. But in the process, I would be dropping a bomb on Emily that could, at best, shake her foundation and, at worst, completely devastate her.

She held me for what seemed like forever. I mean, this was the ugly cry to beat all ugly cries. I was a mess. I suppose that deep down I knew it was going to be a scene. I mean, I don't really care how it looked or what people thought. Still, I'd hoped I would be able to contain the emotional release a little better. Clearly, I couldn't, so I just gave into it and, for the moment, rested comfortably in Emily's arms until my body was ready to cooperate with my mind.

Eventually, I regained my composure. I took a few deep breaths and pulled back so I could look at her. In her expression I saw compassion and love, but also worry and concern.

"Are you okay?"

—"Yeah, let's walk and talk."

At first we did a lot more walking than talking. It wasn't so much that I didn't want to tell her as it was that I quite literally didn't know what to say. I have a much better understanding of it all now, but, at that time, I only knew there was something different about me. So, that's where we started.

> —"Emily, I've got this feeling inside me. There's something different about me."

"OK..."

> —"I've known it since I was a kid. I don't exactly understand it, and that scares the hell out of me... but I can't deny it or hide it any longer. I have to tell you, and I have to figure this out."

"Don, you can tell me anything and we can figure it out together. Tell me what it is."

> —"Well, here's the thing, I'm not exactly sure what 'it' is."

It's pretty ironic that it took so much courage to get me to that moment, only to be at a loss for words. I mean, I'm almost never at a loss for words.

I was ready, she was ready, and yet, I couldn't perform. I suspect that moment of verbal impotence came down to the fact that what I didn't know far surpassed what I did know. What little I knew was largely about how I felt. And feelings are not easily put into words.

My fear finally gave way to frustration. Suddenly, my silence had nothing to do with whether or not to share this part of me with Emily and everything to do with my inability to find the words to adequately express to her what this part of me was.

Emily sensed my frustration and invited me to open up.

> "Just talk to me about your feelings. You don't need to have the perfect words. Just talk to me..."

I took another deep, cleansing breath and stopped worrying about knowing exactly what to say or how it would sound.

> —"I feel like a woman sometimes. Or maybe it's that I feel like a part of me is a woman all the time. I've felt this way for as long as I can remember. I've never known what it means or what to do with it. I kept it hidden my whole life because I felt like it made me 'broken.' I am emotionally exhausted, and I can't carry it alone anymore."

By this time, we'd stopped under one of the pergolas for some rest and shade. I once again took my place seated atop a picnic table, hands clasped in front of me. I dropped my head to wipe away the tears, keenly aware that I was terrified to look up at Emily where she stood across from me.

Forty years of fear, guilt, and shame-induced repression were finally free. I said the words that I was certain I would never ever say. I sat there completely raw, vulnerable, and exposed.

I felt her hand on mine. It gave me the encouragement I needed to look up. Her face was flushed, and her eyes fixed on mine. She was looking through me as much as she was looking at me.

Emily stepped over the bench and sat down next to me. She placed her arm around me and pulled me toward her. I released my tightly clenched hands, turned toward her, and we settled into a comfortable embrace. She squeezed me tightly, and that's where we existed for a little while.

I've always had an immense amount of love, respect, and appreciation for Emily. Simply put, I am grateful for her every minute of every day. In all the times I played out my admission, her reaction, and our conversation, I never once imagined she would be anything less than loving and supportive. So, that begs the question... *Why was I so reluctant to share it with her?*

I absolutely knew Emily would love and support me as an individual. What I didn't know was what my confession would mean for us as a couple and now as a family. I knew that Emily had every right to decide that although she loved me, this was not a journey she could go on with me. That she would have to love and support me in a new and different way. That she could no longer be my spouse. That possibility scared the hell out of me.

> *I wondered if, despite her deep love for me, she would have to let me go.*

Emily squeezed me extra hard and then I felt the tightness of our embrace release. I resisted. I wondered if, despite her deep love for me, she would have to let me go. It was as though I was clinging to her so as not to drift off helplessly into space.

She pulled away more intentionally and looked deep into my eyes.

> "I love you. You're my person. You never have to carry anything alone. Ever."

I cried. She cried. We wiped away our tears. We wiped away each other's tears. We embraced. We kissed. We even shared in the giggles that moments of intense emotion can sometimes give way to. We chatted a little longer and rested comfortably in the moment. We had no idea what this meant for the future, but Emily had made it clear that it was *our* future. She was willing and ready to continue our journey. I remained intimidated by the unknown, but I was exceedingly relieved that I would not have to face it alone.

As we got ready to head home, Emily looked at me quizzically.

> "I'm curious… why did you think that you had to keep this from me all this time and, after almost ten years together, why did you decide to tell me now?"

The answer to Emily's first question initially felt complicated, but it was quite simple. I'd denied and hidden it for so long I'd almost convinced myself that it wasn't even a part of me anymore.

Almost.

For the first forty years of my life, I couldn't conceive of a future in which I was able to be my authentic self. This is who the world expected me to be. This is all I was allowed to do. I was convinced that the path I was relegated to was the only path I would ever walk. Or so I thought.

> *I'd denied and hidden it for so long, I'd almost convinced myself that it wasn't even a part of me anymore.*

The answer to Emily's second question about why – after nearly a decade together – I'd summoned the courage and determination to share this with her, was not a *why* at all. It was a *who*.

It was our daughter, Frankie Marie.

My journey to unapologetic authenticity started when I understood that living an authentic life was not only possible, it was imperative. For Frankie, for me, and as I would come to learn, for everyone in my life.

It all started with that one choice. I committed to doing the hardest thing I had ever done. I had no idea what that would mean or how to successfully navigate the outcome, and it didn't matter. I would figure that out on the journey.

For the first moment in a very long time, I was prepared to trust myself. I was prepared to fight for who I was. I was ready to do what felt right and to show up how I wanted, at all costs.

The compelling reason to embrace authenticity is different for each person, but the first step is the same for everyone. The first uncertain, even perilous step is out of the shadow of conformity and into the light of authenticity.

For me, the next step was letting someone in and showing her who I was. That day in the park with Emily was an act of complete and utter vulnerability. It meant putting myself out there. It meant being ready for her reaction, her response, and whatever came next.

Would she feel betrayed? Would she resent me? Would my truth taint our relationship and contribute to its eventual demise?

These questions and countless more ran on repeat in my head for what felt like every minute of every day. There was no way for me to know how she would react, but no matter what that would look like, she was entitled to it. She had every right to feel whatever she felt, and to make whatever decision she needed to make. That included telling me that she loved me but that she couldn't go on this journey with me. She had every right to say that she was happy for me and that she would support me, but that this was not what she'd signed up for. She could think, feel, react, and process in any way that she saw fit… and I would have to accept it.

I was finally ready to put myself out there in a way I thought I never could. I needed a bridge from where I was to where I wanted to go. The gap seemed impossibly wide and the landscape treacherous.

I desperately needed compassion, encouragement, love, and support. For nearly a decade, Emily and I routinely provided each other with all those things, so I hoped

For the first time in a very long time, I was prepared to trust myself.

she would be the first to help me construct a bridge to self-acceptance and love. Remember, we were partners in business and in life. We had been through struggles and strife together. We survived, overcame, and thrived despite the most difficult of times. This situation felt different, though. All the challenges we faced existed around us; this existed between us. Nevertheless, I put my faith in us and trusted that despite the difference, we would face this together.

In hiding and denying who I was, I had deceived Emily. That realization hit me like a freight train. I acknowledge that it wasn't intentional or malicious; however, the fact remained that I had misled Emily. That was a painful admission and one that I would experience repeatedly with other loved ones.

Although there were countless ways Emily could react when I finally shared my truth with her, I knew with certainty that there was one way she would never respond. She would never react in anger, hatred, or intolerance. She would never meet my vulnerability with negativity.

> *Look for someone who has the psychological flexibility and emotional maturity to understand that this moment is not about them.*

It was in that certainty that I felt safe enough to let her in. If and when you're ready to take this unsure, vulnerable, and terrifying step in your own journey, I encourage you to carefully choose the person or people you let in. Especially at first. Love may not always be the best criteria. Look for someone who also has the psychological flexibility and emotional maturity to understand that this vulnerable moment isn't about them.

In this moment, you'll need them to be there for you, without hesitation. They get to start feeling and processing what it means for them and how they want to respond, but only after they hold you, hug you, and make you feel seen and safe. Just like Emily did for me.

If you don't feel like you have an Emily in your life, come find me. I'll be your Emily.

When you choose well, letting someone in will support you in your journey to unconditional self-love and unapologetic authenticity in a variety of ways. If, like me, you have been encumbered by the weight of all you've been carrying, this person can step in and lighten your load. Letting Emily in was a relief of epic proportions.

I felt uneasy, exposed, and vulnerable. Her kindness, compassion, patience, and support were everything at a time when I needed them the most.

> Letting Emily in was a relief of epic proportions.

She'd willingly shouldered the burden of my journey before I was ready to come out without so much as a complaint or cross word. She'd created a safe space for me to exist. That's something I'll never forget and can't adequately thank her for, no matter how hard I try. I welcomed her into what felt like my own private hell, and she eagerly ran into the fire for me.

I always believed it was my responsibility to make life easier and better for Emily... but there I was doing exactly the opposite. That's a hard acknowledgment.

Once again, I came face to face with the fallout that had me seeking shelter for all those years. This time was different though, because I wasn't alone anymore. Emily and I would face the fear of the fallout together. She showed me that many, if not most, of the things I feared were only real in my imagination. She proved to me that even if some of those fears did manifest, it wouldn't matter, because we would always have each other.

She accepted and loved the real me. She walked beside me through it all because she believed I was worth it. Even before I did.

It took an excruciatingly long time to finally let someone in. That felt like a hard-earned, impressive milestone. I was proud of how far I had come, eternally grateful for who I was with, and yet I couldn't help but feel there were mountains still to climb.

When I first spoke with Emily, I knew very little about who I was and what I wanted. I held tight to the things that felt right to me. The *real* me.

I was no longer committed to satisfying the wants and needs of a judgmental society that refused to see, accept, or understand me. After letting Emily in, she and I worked together to create safe spaces where I could listen quietly to my heart and act in alignment with it. I worked hard to pay attention to things that I previously ignored and dismissed.

I intentionally shared all my thoughts and feelings with her. It amazed me just how frequently I noticed something that provided insight into the real me. I began consuming content at a remarkable pace. Some items focused specifically on the topic of gender while others more broadly provided insight regarding individuality and authenticity. I was finally able to find representation that was positive, healthy, and affirming.

> *Yet I couldn't help but feel there were mountains still to climb.*

I steadily unearthed who I truly was and abandoned who I had been convinced I needed to be. I did more of what I wanted and less of what was expected. I accepted that I was special, unique, and different. I finally understood that *different* doesn't mean *broken*.

5

DIFFERENT DOESN'T MEAN BROKEN

> "All young people, regardless of sexual orientation or identity, deserve a safe and supportive environment in which to achieve their full potential."
>
> —*Harvey Milk*

Being the kind and loving spouse that she is, Emily was quick to support me in both words and action. She consistently checked in to see how I was doing and what I was thinking. She said the most caring and comforting things. And, on occasion and based on my revelations, she ordered items she felt would support me as I explored my gender identity and expression.

Early on, I was incredibly self-conscious and asked for privacy when trying on traditionally feminine clothes, accessories, or makeup. Despite telling Emily my truth, I was not quite able to share this with her.

Although I very much appreciated her efforts, I started to notice an exhausting pattern. I would steel my nerves and summon my mental and emotional strength to try on whatever beautiful thing she had bought for me. I'd apply some makeup and accessorize to the best of my meager ability. Then I would step in front of the mirror and, in an instant, the voices would start.

> **"You look so stupid. People are going to laugh at you. This is going to make Emily and Frankie's lives harder."**

Then, I would cry. The words from those mean, hateful, judgmental voices would win.

I'd change, wash my face, and rejoin Emily downstairs. She would ask if I'd liked the item, if it fit, or if she needed to exchange it for another size or color. Sadness would wash over me, and tears would overwhelm the moment. I'd simply say, "I can't talk about it right now."

Then one day, long into my journey… I finally managed to break this cycle.

On one unremarkable afternoon, something truly remarkable happened. I put on clothes that Emily had purchased for me and once again stepped in front of the mirror with the dread that I'd become surprisingly accustomed to. The voices started up, louder and meaner than ever. I felt the tears rise up and spill over. But this time there was something different about them. They were less the tears of sorrow and more the tears of frustration, and dare I say, anger. For the first time, I stepped closer to the mirror and fixed my gaze in deep defiance of the thing that had a hold on me for as long as I can remember.

> *I felt the tears rise up and spill over. But this time there was something different about them.*

And then it happened. I *felt* something. Something profound. Something comforting. Something hopeful. Those relentless voices that so frequently engaged in an all-out assault on me were quiet. At least for the moment.

When I stood there amidst the silence, looking in that mirror, a sense of joy, calm, and contentment washed over me. It was all-encompassing and euphoric. In that new moment, I saw and accepted the real me for the first time.

I couldn't help but smile.

The voice in my head eventually returned to break the silence. I got ready to defend myself from another onslaught of negativity and self-loathing, but there was no need. This time was different. The voice was calm and soothing. I felt it as much as I heard it. The voice inside my head simply said:

"There you are."

It confirmed what I already knew in my heart – what Emily had helped me understand for the first time. We discovered together that *this is me*. I am valid. And I am beautiful.

Even in this place, my safest space, I struggled with authenticity and contentment. I remained full of uncertainty and fear. I was more fragile than ever. Despite the outpouring of unconditional love and support from Emily as I explored my gender identity and expression, I remained embarrassed of who I was, what I wanted, and what felt right for me. Nevertheless, I persisted.

> *This time the voice inside my head simply said, "There you are."*

In the early days of my exploration, thrift stores were a great place to experiment with fashion. These stores tended to be large with few shoppers – which was exactly what I needed. I was still embarrassed and worried about what others might think. The employees were nice, and they were attentive. But not too attentive. The last thing I wanted back then was attention.

In the event I got a "look," or someone questioned the clothes I wanted to try on, I had all sorts of stories ready. I was preparing for Halloween. I was buying a little something for my wife. I was participating in a charity event and we were doing a fun skit. The longer the look or the more pressing the questions, the more elaborate my story.

It didn't really matter if they believed me – which I am sure they didn't most of the time. It was enough for me to have a cover story ready to reassure my delicate psyche and protect my demanding ego.

So, here and there, I started buying more traditionally feminine clothing. A couple dollars for a skirt or a blouse was a reasonable expense to affirm my gender identity and explore my gender expression. I was still too embarrassed and insecure to bring Emily along on these shopping excursions. I struggled to even show her what I bought when I got home.

> *I ever so slowly inched toward alignment between who I was and how I showed up.*

That didn't matter so much as the acknowledgment that with each venture, I ever so slowly inched toward alignment between who I was and how I showed up.

I had taken a leap forward toward unwavering self-acceptance, unconditional self-love, and unapologetic authenticity. I knew now that achieving these long-coveted beliefs was not only possible, it was inevitable.

Although I always knew there was something different about me... something *unique*, something *special*... sadly, I didn't see myself as special or unique. In my head and in my heart, "different" meant "broken," so that's what I saw, and that's what I felt. Broken! I buried my *unique* and hid my *special* from everyone.

On the outside, I was happy, confident, and successful. I had gotten great at being who I was supposed to be, doing what I was allowed to do, and achieving what was expected of me. I ticked all those boxes, and in the eyes of others, I fit conveniently into one of their containers. I was right where they thought I belonged.

Tragically, there was no container big enough or just right for the real me. Instead, I was only a fraction of what my heart and soul yearned to become. What was expected of me was far below – and just a bit outside – what I was truly capable of. The idea of an audacious, authentic existence that thumbed its nose at conventional expectation was terrifying. I learned to suppress and compress the things about me that didn't fit. I squeezed into a container, any container, no matter how awkward or uncomfortable.

Although every day wasn't the same, I lived under a looming cloud of fear, carrying the weight of my secret.

When was it that you started to believe it wasn't okay to be who you are? Did it hit you like a bolt of lightning one day, or did it slowly grow over time like flood waters rising from pouring rain?

> *I lived under a looming cloud of fear, carrying the weight of my secret.*

Who introduced you to the idea that something about your core identity was not okay? Who made you believe that it was shameful, harmful, or even sinful? What did they say, and how did they say it? Did they even know when they were talking *near* you or *to* you that they were also talking *about* you? How did that make you feel?

If your seemingly dirty little secret was still safe, did you fearfully and understandably betray who you are, nodding your head and playing along? If you'd already shared your truth, did you find yourself exposed and afraid? Were you subjected to a painful emotional, psychological, or even physical assault by someone who could have – should have – seen and loved you unconditionally for who you are?

I realize that my current level of self-confidence and unapologetic authenticity is pretty much off the charts, but it wasn't always that way. I didn't always see my uniqueness as a superpower. I suffered the same insecurities as anyone, maybe more than most.

I hid what I thought was broken for a very long time. The negative impact of that suppression was insidious and painful, but I never much worried about how to fix it. Looking back now, I'm not certain why I didn't work harder to figure myself out. Maybe it's because I believed I was broken beyond repair. Maybe it was because I was a big fat chicken and so ashamed that I didn't want to see who I really was. Maybe it was because I was so embarrassed and disappointed in myself that I felt unworthy of the effort it would take. Maybe I was so intimidated by even the thought of everything it would take that I was paralyzed to do anything at all.

It's like something out of the movie *Inception*. The more ashamed and embarrassed I felt, the more ashamed and embarrassed I became. The crippling negative emotions doubled time and time again. I went deeper into denial. Despite the depths of my denial, I also knew that I wasn't actually broken. I was different... but different doesn't mean broken. Since you can't fix something, or more accurately *someone*, who isn't broken, there's no use trying.

> *Despite the depths of my denial, I also knew that I wasn't actually broken.*

That was a monumental realization for me. I was convinced that different was the equivalent of broken. Nope. I was unique and special, and there was nothing wrong with that, nothing wrong with me.

Different isn't something to be ashamed of. It's not something to be hidden away or exiled.

I wasn't broken... but something was. It was that I'd believed that I was broken. I had been convinced that the rigid, outdated, and short-sighted rules applied to me. I hadn't realized that I never needed to follow those rules in the first place. They were irrelevant to me. The idea that I was living every day constrained by what I thought was expected and permitted was despicable. Ironically, the constraints that I allowed to be placed on who I was and what I did had nothing to do with me. They were about a society desperate to control and limit what I was capable of. It was about a society too terrified of what I represented.

As a young person, I believed in and surrendered my identity to a common false dichotomy – the gender binary. Much like the rules I thought I needed to follow, the notion that gender is binary is rooted in outdated, short-sighted science. Comprehensive medical research has shown us that gender is far more complex than an either/or label assigned to you based solely on the parts you're born with. The intricacies of human gender can't be reduced to just this or that. Humans are beautiful, complex, multi-faceted creatures.

When I started my journey, I had no idea where the path would take me. I knew there was something different about me, but I genuinely had no idea what that really meant or who I truly was. Seriously, no idea. I was searching for guidance that would help me understand, guidance that would help me grapple with the thoughts and feelings I'd had since I was a kid.

I was scared and confused. I didn't know how to process what I was thinking and feeling. Despite my recent discovery about who I was, and my commitment to authenticity, I remained in the shadow of fear, guilt, shame, and doubt. I acknowledged that I was different and that different didn't mean broken, but I had only just started to explore what that meant. I realized that despite Emily's support and my personal commitment to authenticity, my identity was still unacceptable to much of the world around me.

I was a little boy (or at least that's what I was assigned at birth) who liked to wear a satin skirt. It made me feel pretty. It affirmed who I was. It just felt right. According to others, though, it was wrong. It didn't matter if it felt right to me. I wasn't allowed to be who I was or want what I wanted.

At that impressionable age I had no idea who I was. And I figured it was fruitless to try and figure it out because the label I placed on that particular part of me was "broken." I was still ashamed and embarrassed by it. And what typically happens to things that are broken? They get hidden away with all the other useless things, unlikely to be fixed or serve a beneficial purpose. Worse yet, they are discarded altogether. Thrown out with the garbage. Far too many people engage in self-harm because they believe it's their only option. They're convinced they're not valuable, worthy, or "enough." They believe that just because they're different, that something is wrong with them. In actuality, they're priceless and precious. They get to be seen, accepted, understood, and loved unconditionally.[1]

After decades of repression and denial, the idea of choosing unapologetic authenticity introduced a whole new set of challenges. I had no idea who I really was, no idea how to figure it out, and no idea what it would mean. Although I finally understood that different didn't mean I needed to be fixed, I was woefully unprepared for whatever might be next. I had no idea where this road would lead.

Despite my confusion, I was determined to move forward holding on to what little clarity I did have. I was absolutely certain that in order to discover who I was, how I wanted to show up, and how I wanted the world to see me, I would need to restructure my self-constructed systems. I would need to consider everything I had learned, challenge all that I thought I knew, and evaluate what I had come to believe. All of this in the hopes that I could learn to see myself. Love myself. Be proud of myself.

It was time to stop thinking, and to start feeling.

I was prepared to embark on this wild ride, and I would use my hope for unconditional self-love and unapologetic authenticity to light the path. I was finally ready to start the exhausting journey toward who I was destined to become.

I knew what it felt like to pretend to be something that I was not. I knew it was time to stop listening to the nasty self-defeating

---

[1] Help is available. If you or someone you know is facing mental health struggles or emotional distress, the 988 Lifeline offers caring counselors around the clock by phone, text, or online chat. http://988lifeline.org

voices in my head. I knew I didn't want to feel like that anymore. It was time to start paying closer attention to how I felt in my heart. It was time to stop thinking, and to start feeling.

Just like that little kid in my aunt's basement, I was going to try to be blissfully unaware of other people's opinions. I would no longer be concerned about what other people thought was right. I was no longer going to worry about what I was allowed to do, or what was expected of me. Gone were the days of avoiding the fallout by staying in the shelter I had confined myself to for so long.

I was no longer compelled to choose conformity to find safety. It was time to find safety in the people who were ready to show up and stand up for me in all my authentic glory… to cleave to those who would accept, love, support, and celebrate who I was rather than punish or banish me for it.

When I'd looked into that mirror and the mean voices in my head were silenced by a feeling of contentment, I knew that my mind and heart were finally falling into alignment. They were at last conspiring to set me on my path to clarity. What I didn't know then but quickly learned is that this journey was not going to be a stroll down a flower-lined path. No, it was more of a gauntlet fit only for the fierce and brave.

I don't want to scare or intimidate you, but I do want you to get started with your eyes wide open. Know that achieving this level of contentment may just be the hardest thing you'll ever do, but it will also likely be the most rewarding. I can tell you from personal experience that it's an absolute game changer.

Just think about all the energy you've spent hiding or denying things about yourself. Consider for a moment all that fear, guilt shame, and doubt that have negatively impacted your life… all the ways they've compelled you to question your worth and what you're capable of… how they've stopped you from chasing your dreams and creating the life you've always wanted.

It's long past time for you to find your freedom, so let's get started.

The Process

Now that your head and your heart are working together, the rest is going to come naturally, right? Nope. You've been conditioned to operate as you have for as long as you can remember. You learned all those things, and now you get to unlearn them. And that's going to take time and effort. This means you get to manage your expectations and offer yourself plenty of grace and considerable latitude as you make your way through the gauntlet.

This process isn't linear. It's a squiggly zigzag circular mess from start to finish. Just when you think you have it all figured out, something will change. The universe will throw you a curveball, and you'll get to reassess, recalibrate, and accommodate. No matter what happens, you must remain committed. You must not lose sight of who you are and who you're becoming. This is your relentless pursuit of authenticity and contentment.

> *This process isn't linear. It's a squiggly zigzag circular mess from start to finish.*

How is it that I could move ever so slowly toward authenticity, contentment, and utter freedom yet feel more uncertain and fragile with each step?

That's just how this works. If you ever climbed trees as a kid, it's kind of like stepping out onto a tree branch. The further you move away from the safety of the tree's trunk, the more unsupported you become. And rightfully so, because there is nothing to hold onto, and as the branch narrows it feels less stable.

That leaves you with no trunk to hold onto and a branch that could snap at any moment. It's a delicate process. You get to renegotiate with each step as you find your footing. You get to establish your balance and estimate just how far you can venture out before the branch breaks.

You won't always get it right. I know I didn't. I miscalculated a number of times. I heard the branch crack and so I ran back to the trunk more times than I can count. On a few occasions, I pushed too far too fast. The branch gave way, and I fell hard to the unforgiving ground. But I survived, and you will too. Remember that person or those people that you let in? The ones who will not judge you. The ones who accept, love, and support you. The ones with whom you feel safe. Those are the ones who will be standing below you watching, waiting, ready to catch you should you fall.

You don't need to wait until you have it all figured out. You don't need to have the perfect language. You don't need to know exactly what you want to say, how to say it, or exactly what it means. Find the person or people who will listen to what you're ready to tell them – through the sobs, the gasps, and the ugly crying. Find the people who are willing and able to go on the long hard journey with you to help and support you as you figure it all out. Pick the person or people you feel the safest with and include them by being transparent and vulnerable like never before.

You don't need to wait until you have it all figured out.

These people will aid you on your journey by offering something that you may not be ready or able to give yourself. They will offer you the gift of someone seeing, accepting, and loving you for who you are. Your first ever experience with unwavering acceptance and unconditional love may come from someone else.

Sometimes other people in your life will be more accepting and understanding of you than you are of yourself. They will see things differently than you do because they do not have the same experiences, traumas, and internalized phobias. Your people will show you that something you thought was inconceivable is actually possible. They will teach you how to accept and embrace yourself by accepting and embracing you first.

I slowly found the strength and courage to step out further a little bit at a time. I shared more of my personal journey with Emily. Safety and comfort were a consideration in every decision I made. So, it only made sense that my next step would take place at home with her, because that's where I felt the safest.

Emily knew I was exploring my identity and expression. She routinely bought me clothing and I was shopping too, despite knowing I still wasn't ready to try any of these items on in front of her.

I would wear my new clothes around the house when she was out. I hated that the part of me I was learning to accept and embrace still felt like a dirty little secret when it came to her.

When she was out, Emily had a habit of calling to let me know how her day was going and when she would be home. That wasn't new or different, but these calls now served a slightly different purpose. She was calling as a way of respecting my privacy and boundaries. She was letting me know when she would be home so that I could change if I wanted to.

And I always wanted to.

I was too insecure to show her this part of me... yet. The thought of it made me terribly anxious and emotional. I wanted it so badly, but I just couldn't find the strength and courage it took to be completely vulnerable, even with Emily. Which, incidentally, had nothing to do with her and everything to do with me.

Over time, I began to show her what I found on my little thrift store treasure hunts. I laid out how I envisioned the outfits coming together. I asked for her feedback since she has impeccable taste and an amazing sense of style.

At first glance, this may appear to be a small step, but it really was a massive leap forward. In classic Emily fashion (pun intended), she was committed to helping me learn about all the things. She assembled a small makeup kit for me, a kind and affirming gesture, again letting me know that she loved me and that I was safe with her.

I'm sure she could tell I was insecure and nervous about wearing any of it. She offered to teach me about the different products and explain how to use them while she applied her own makeup. It was such a comforting way to learn. Eventually I learned to apply the products myself with her guidance, and before long, I was a seasoned pro at putting on my face and powdering my nose.

She taught me the fashion basics – layering, patterns, textiles – and dressing for my body type and skin tone. She was supportive but also candid with me about my finds. I learned that some of the things I thought were treasure were really trash. They weren't the right cut and accentuated less flattering features. The colors were not the best for my skin tone. The patterns or styles were frequently outdated. My record wasn't the best but how I was doing didn't matter. What mattered to me was that I was finally doing it.

It felt like adolescence all over again.

I was learning something entirely new, so a few mistakes were to be expected. It felt a little like adolescence all over again. But I was finding my groove and deciding what my vibe was going to be. The glaring difference was that – for the first time in my life – I didn't allow external influences or social pressure to tell me what I was allowed to wear. I got to choose what I wore, and I got to be unapologetically authentic about how I expressed myself. I was determined to decide those things for myself.

Emily was the model of patience, respect, and understanding. She never expressed frustration or exasperation. She never pushed. She gently supported and encouraged me every step of the way.

I called her to check in and see how her day was coming along. She said not to worry, that she would be out for a while and would let me know before she came home. Later that day, as promised, she called to let me know she was on her way and would be home shortly.

I remember sitting on our stairs in my thrift store skirt as we engaged in customary married couple small talk. I was of course interested in how her day was, what I would prepare for dinner, and whatever else happened to come up, but I was really stalling so I could work up the courage to ask her something that I had been fixated on all day.

As our conversation trailed off, I sensed that she was getting ready to say goodbye. I promised myself I wouldn't chicken out. I sheepishly told Emily that I didn't plan on changing before she got home... and I wanted to know if that would be okay with her. She reassured me that it was just fine, that she loved me, and that she would see me soon.

The time between when we finished the call and when the garage door opened felt like an exceedingly long thirty minutes. I paced the floor, wringing my hands, feeling anticipation and anxiety in equal measure.

Emily walked in with a few bags from the grocery store. She set them on the counter before she turned to me and handed me a bouquet of flowers. She told me that she loved me and that I looked beautiful.

I don't think I will ever feel as loved and beautiful as I did in that moment.

I don't think I will ever feel as loved and as beautiful as I did in that moment.

She gave me a hug, squeezing me tightly before she let go. She followed it with a kiss and a request that I please help her put away the groceries, since that's what we would have normally done, and this was our new normal. This experience represented a turning point in my existence. This was the start of something new and beautiful. This was the start of my authentic era.

Let me tell you, it was hard work – one of hardest things I'd ever done. I had a lifetime of fear, guilt, shame, and doubt to rid myself of and that wasn't going to happen overnight. The process of unlearning all that conditioning took time and effort.

It was intimidating to stare into a future so radically different and uncertain. It was like living in "Bizarro World," the fictional cube-shaped planet of Htrae (Earth spelled backward, so clever). It was initially introduced by DC Comics in the late 1960s and re-popularized in the eighth season of *Seinfeld* in the 1990s. On Htrae, everything is opposite. Up is down, left is right, good is bad... you get the idea. I was about to challenge everything I'd ever learned and test every boundary I'd ever set. In my new Bizarro World, something that was previously inconceivable was suddenly not only a possibility but a certainty.

There are a number of things you can likely expect on your journey that I experienced on mine:

- It doesn't happen quickly.
- It isn't easy.
- You aren't going to get it right the first time... or all the time.

Remember, this whole process is a squiggly zigzag circular mess. Some things you try are going to work and others won't. Some things will fit and others won't. Sometimes you're going to feel so much better while other times you're going to feel quite a bit worse. What matters most is that you remain true to yourself and act in alignment with exactly who you are as often as you can. Use your commitment to unconditional self-love and unapologetic authenticity to light your path.

Be patient and kind to yourself. Be prepared to give yourself grace and lead with compassion. You are learning something entirely new. It's both hard and complicated at first, but I promise it will get easier and simpler with time and deliberate practice.

The Reward

Eventually you'll find that the times when things don't work, don't fit, and have you feeling bad will be less frequent. You'll learn from them and get better at all this. The times when things work really well, fit comfortably, and have you feeling oh so good will become more frequent. Contentment will eventually become the status quo. Ultimately, you're going to replace confusion with clarity as you figure out who you are and how you want to show up.

Take it from the person who could barely stand to see themselves in the mirror in a skirt or dress who eventually went on to walk the red carpet at The Knot Worldwide Annual Gala in Manhattan in the sexiest asymmetrical sequin gown and chiffon skirt with four-inch black heels. And let me tell you, it had been an intimidating road from that bedroom mirror to the red carpet. You too will get from where you are to where you want to go with patience and perseverance.

I steadily continued to navigate my way from who I'd allowed myself to be, to the person I really am. It was uncomfortable and unpredictable. Sometimes I was making steady progress and other times I was completely stalled out. Every once in a while, I even made massive progress in a relatively short span of time.

I tried not to focus on the quantity of time or the amount of progress. How much I was able to accomplish and how long it took was frequently self-defeating. Instead, I focused on the quality of my effort and commitment.

I discovered what I like to call *net progress*. It's more common than ever to set unrealistic expectations for yourself. If you don't progress as quickly or efficiently as you think you should, or wished you would, the focus of your energy gets directed at "shoulding all over yourself." You *should* be doing better. You *should* be further along. And on and on and on. All this does is have you feeling bad about yourself, bringing your progress to a screeching halt. It casts a long shadow of doubt over you and your journey. It's annoying and frustrating. It's also perfectly common. It's all a part of the process. Beating yourself up is self-defeating and futile. You get to manage your expectations and realize the process is messy. You get to accept that you're doing your best and that's all you can do.

Your goal isn't flawless progress toward unattainable perfection. All you need is *net progress*. At each milestone you get closer to your goal rather than farther away. That doesn't mean that you never backslide or veer off course; it's not a matter of if but when that inevitably happens. Being okay with that will help you give yourself the grace and latitude you deserve. You get to keep things positive and moving in the right direction.

After all the up and down and back and forth and this way and that way, the most productive expectation you can have is net progress that you get to celebrate.

If you haven't achieved net progress, you get to reflect on your recent achievements and setbacks. Consider if and how you got off course. Reevaluate your effort and commitment. Refocus your attention on what feels right and those things that are in alignment with who you are. Ensure you're doing your best. You'll once again be headed toward your ultimate goals of unwavering self-acceptance, unconditional self-love, and unapologetic authenticity.

> *Your goal isn't flawless progress toward unattainable perfection.*

So there I was, learning about fashion, exploring my gender identity, and developing my own sense of style and personal expression. Although it still wasn't easy and it didn't really feel natural, I was doing it... and that was something special.

All of that was completely inconceivable not long ago. At this point, I was only brave enough to share it with Emily, my immediate family, and a very small group of close friends. These were my people. I felt seen and safe with them. I continued to rely on how I felt to silence those ever-so-mean voices inside my head. I knew I was on the right track. I was routinely overcome with joy and contentment. These emotions returned more and more frequently and stayed longer with each visit. Self-acceptance, love, and authenticity were finally becoming a part of me and the result was joy, contentment, and a host of other positive emotions. Although I didn't know it (and likely wouldn't have believed it), there would soon come a time when those emotions would never leave. They would remain with me and create an overwhelming feeling of euphoria.

With increased exploration and deliberate practice came comfort. As I got more proficient, I got more efficient. Eventually, it became quite fun to feel this good. It was refreshing to see myself for who I am, not who I'd allowed myself to be. That was progress worth celebrating.

It was time to consider what was next for me so I could inch ever so slowly and cautiously forward. That's exactly how I would describe my progress. Slow and cautious. As I considered what came next, there were no obvious choices or clear paths. Each new step was a leap of faith. The only way to determine if it was a good or bad fit was to jump.

Each new step was a leap of faith.

Seeing as how all this was new to me, my leaps may have been more like bunny hops. That didn't matter. They were my bunny hops. What mattered most is that I was leaping and hopping every day.

I was still very much aware of and intimidated by the idea of the fallout. My authentic identity and expression are in clear defiance of social and cultural norms. Labels are what you might call a "necessary evil." I'm not a big fan of them but I can admit that they do serve a purpose. Labels provide an opportunity to survey and sum up who you are and how you want to be seen by others.

These labels create a shortcut that captures and communicates your essence as well as what you identify *with* and *as*. Where most go wrong is underestimating the validity and importance of self-constructed labels and overestimating the validity and importance of those labels created for and assigned to them by others.

Externally created and assigned labels are an extension of other people's opinions. There is often an abundance of ignorance, oversimplification, fear, judgment, and control baked into those sentiments. When it comes to your labels, the only thing other people are responsible for is accepting and respecting them. This gets to be the absolute bare minimum cost of admission into your life – a nonnegotiable boundary that you create and protect.

Ideally, the people in your life are committed to you. They will love you unconditionally and immeasurably. These are both critical, because *how* they love you is equally, if not more important, than *how much* they love you. They willingly invest time and resources so they can accept, understand, respect, and appreciate everything about you. Tragically, that's not always the case. As you grow, evolve, adapt, and live authentically, some people in your life will be unwilling to see and accept who you are and who you become.

I've had quite a rude awakening that I'm confident isn't unique to my story and journey. I was seriously disappointed by some of the people in my life. I understand that adjusting and accepting new and different things takes time. I also know there is a direct correlation between the time it takes and the degree to which things are new and different. I was sharing something relatively shocking, so I managed my expectations. I was full of hope, and I was prepared to be patient. What I was not prepared for was apathy, intolerance and, worst of all, abandonment.

Labels are an extension of other people's opinions.

Just as I was on my journey, the people in my life were on theirs. My audacious, authentic identity was radically different. Nevertheless, I was confident that the relationships we had forged would eventually allow others to be there for me after the initial shock wore off. If I just waited the requisite amount of time, they would adjust to the real me – not the new me, the real me. Surely, the people I'd always accepted would be prepared to do the same. They would strive to understand and accept who I was. The people that I loved unconditionally would express their love for the real me. The people I'd relentlessly supported through job losses, career changes, death, and divorce would empathize and offer compassion for the years of pain and anguish I'd endured. The people that I'd fought with and for – to ensure their voices were heard and that they had the same rights as everyone else – would acknowledge that because of my gender identity, I was a target for bigotry, hatred, and violence. I believed they would see that I was under attack, and they would protect, defend, and fight for me.

Some of the people proved me right while others proved me very wrong.

Maya Angelou is famous for inspiring the world with her beautiful words. One of her most famous quotes reads: "When someone shows you who they are, believe them." This was her elegant way of saying that actions speak louder than words, and that making excuses for how other people act is an exercise in futility.

The person you harm most when you compromise who you are, or when you make excuses for others, is you. My expectations for the people in my life didn't matter as much as their commitment and their intentions. I learned rather quickly and painfully that those I had the highest expectations for often fell the furthest short. Ironically, many of those for whom I had relatively low expectations far exceeded them.

> *Actions speak louder than words, and making excuses for how other people act is an exercise in futility.*

I know you might be thinking that maybe my expectations were askew. Maybe. Or maybe not.

I believed there was a direct correlation between the tenure and strength of a relationship. Essentially, the longer I knew someone, the more deeply rooted and strong our relationship should be, and the more confident I could be in their support and acceptance.

Nope. That was not at all the reality. Despite considerable effort and evaluation, I couldn't really make sense of it all. There was no discernable pattern.

I couldn't figure out how to adjust my expectations in a way that led to less disappointment and heartache. I was confused at every turn. People who had been a fixture in my life for years hardly acknowledged the real me. They infrequently asked questions to understand me better. They rarely expressed their love and support amidst my turmoil. Some people said all the right things

– or at least the things they thought they were supposed to say – while others didn't really say or do much of anything at all.

Maybe there were elements of their belief system that they were unwilling to challenge. Maybe they thought I was stupid, embarrassing, or even dangerous. Maybe they were just uncomfortable. Maybe they didn't want to feel awkward or ignorant by admitting they didn't know what they didn't know. Maybe they thought the best thing to do was act nonchalant like it wasn't a big deal and that it didn't matter.

The reality is that it was a really big deal, and it matters a lot. It's *me*. It's who I am. It's finally finding the courage to be exactly who I am, everywhere I go, no matter who I'm with.

It's not about saying or doing what others think I'm supposed to say or do. It's not my responsibility to be convenient or help them feel comfortable. It's not really about them at all. It's about me. It's about their commitment to seeing me, accepting me, understanding me, respecting me, loving me, and supporting me.

> *We have zero control over the thoughts, feelings, or behavior of others.*

Now that I've learned how to set and hold fast to my boundaries, I've seen the positive impact it's had on my life. It's become my new standard. Previously I might have said that this was my minimum expectation, but I've learned that setting expectations for others is problematic. Sure, I can set expectations all day long, but I can't force people to care about them. It's entirely up to them to meet or exceed those expectations. It's a problematic pattern and a breeding ground for disappointment. It's also another reminder that we have zero control over the thoughts, feelings, or behavior of others.

I'm going to take a huge piece of metaphorical chalk and draw a line on the ground. Once I do, there are three elements present. There's your side, their side and, of course, the chalk line.

Everything on your side of the line is within your sphere of influence and locus of control. Everything on their side of that chalk line is someone else's domain.

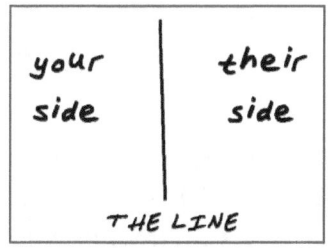

You get to acknowledge and accept that you have no control over their side. Moreover, it would be a waste of your time and effort to try. Equally, that means that nobody else gets to have control on your side of the line.

The final element in this equation – the chalk line – represents your boundaries. They are based on the absolute minimum standard you set to comfortably invite someone over to your side of the line. If they cannot meet this set of requirements, then they are not welcome.

Each new person you meet has a chalk line of their very own that serves as their "price of admission." That's because no two people are identical. Therefore, each of us has a set of standards and boundaries that are unique.

Extending an invitation to come over to your side is a big, huge, *massive* deal. When you allow someone in, you've decided to trust them. You believe they are safe enough to welcome them into your life.

Now, just because this person has ventured onto your side of the line doesn't mean you've given them the keys to the kingdom. They don't have control over you or your "stuff." However, once you invite them over, you're also welcoming their thoughts, feelings, and behavior into your world. You've decided to open yourself to their influence and they will undoubtedly have an impact on you.

My minimum standard for everyone – regardless of how close or far they are from my core – is considerable now. It wasn't always that way. I used to be quite capricious with my boundaries. I pretty much let anyone and everyone come and go as they pleased. I wanted to fit in, and I craved a sense of belonging. I was desperate for acceptance and approval, so my standards were practically nonexistent.

Desperate for all these things, I betrayed who I was for who I thought others wanted me to be... with dire consequences. I lost sight of who I was, and I abandoned the opportunity to become who I was destined to be.

Tragically, along with my metaphorical chalk lines, I was being erased from existence. Or so I thought. It turns out it wasn't my existence that was threatened, it was my visibility. Call it what you will, I was being erased just the same.

I spent so much time denying who I was that I eventually lost sight of myself. I never developed my true identity because the idea of being my authentic self was inconceivable.

Not knowing who you are sucks. It creates endless problems that are complicated and frustrating. If you yourself don't know who you are, it's impossible to show others the real you. And if you can't show others the real you, then all you can do is show the world what it wants to see. That means whatever the world sees isn't you at all. You're a fake. A phony. A fugazi. A chalk outline that represents where your authentic self ceased to exist.

The world wants and needs something, anything, it can place its labels on. It wants you to fit into its categories and containers. It wants you to accept what it tells you. It wants you to believe you are what it says you are. Much like in the 1999 classic *The Matrix*, the world wants you to take the "blue" pill. The world will allow you to exist... but only inside the matrix. Your only reality is the one that's been constructed for you.

Knowing exactly who you are can suck too, but in a very different way. Taking the "red" pill rips you violently from your constructed reality and you find yourself fighting for your identity and existence. If you recall, life outside the matrix was no picnic for Morpheus, Neo and the others. When Lana and Lilly Wachowski created Zion – the dark and dreary fictional region outside the matrix – they perfectly depicted the hellish existence of a person who rejected conformity and fought for authenticity. As trans women, their inspiration for the *Matrix* trilogy was deeply personal. The movies were rooted in hope and, although they admitted the world wasn't ready for it at the time, they recently confirmed these movies were designed as a trans allegory. It was their intention to represent what it's like to live your life outside the typical bounds of a conventional society.

Being unique is something that every human shares. Ironically, individuality is rarely rewarded. In fact, the world routinely punishes people for being different.

What an unenviable position. You finally discover who you are and courageously prepare to share that with the world only to stop short of authentic expression. Despite your best efforts, you just can't summon the courage needed to face your fear of the fallout. You can't help but fixate on what other people will think, what other people will say, and what other people will do when they meet the new, real, authentic you. So, you don't. You can't. The fear, doubt, guilt, and shame set in. You decide once again that the fallout will be too great.

If you just show the world what it wants to see – in alignment with its categories, containers, and labels – then you can fit in. You imagine it will be better to spare yourself and your loved ones the embarrassment and discomfort of going against the grain.

Better for who? And at what cost?

Turns out it's not better for anyone, and the cost is exorbitant.

I realize I'm not giving you much opportunity for hope, but there is a light at the end of the tunnel. In fact, there's a completely different train you get to hop on. On this train, there are no long dark tunnels that force you to question who you are or who you're allowed to be. On this train, you're the engineer. You may not know everything, but you know that it's your train and you get to decide where you are, where you're going, how fast you'll go, and maybe even how you'll get there.

It's time for you to discover and accept who you are – to courageously choose authenticity and reject conformity. It's time to turn that chalk outline into a living, breathing, three-dimensional version of you. Save the chalk to establish your boundaries.

Not knowing who you are sucks pretty bad. But knowing who you are, yet lacking the confidence and courage to be that person, sucks worse. All that's left then is to discover who you are while you build the confidence and find the courage to boldly choose authenticity over conformity. To love yourself unconditionally. To resist doubt and reject hesitation.

Authenticity demands a lot from you.

When I put it like that, it seems so easy... but it's not. It's nowhere close to easy. In fact, it's one of the hardest things you'll ever do. I really want you to sit with that for a moment because I genuinely mean it. Authenticity demands a lot from you. It needs all your strength, courage, pride, and commitment to resist the considerable pressure to conform.

Despite all this, I still believe in you, and I know you can do it. The reason I know you can do it is because I did it. There are a great many things about me that are special, but there's no magical bit that makes me more capable of this than you. There is however a super special magical trick that you'll absolutely need to get started. In an effort to manage your expectations a bit, I want you to know that this won't make the process any easier, but it will make it easier to get started. Once you take the first step, you'll see the potential and feel the power of your authenticity. Momentum will begin to build, and before you know it, you'll really be moving.

So what's the catalyst that's going to kick off the process? It's really quite simple (but not necessarily easy). It all starts with you accepting that unapologetic authenticity is a choice. *Your choice.*

It's simple because it's entirely up to you. You get to choose if and when you will take that first step away from conformity and toward authenticity.

Outside factors can influence you, but ultimately the locus of control is one hundred percent inside you. Maybe you've been reluctant to make the bold decision to step fully into who you are because you suspect some people in your life are not ready for the real you. Maybe you fear they will sit somewhere on the spectrum between unsupportive and outright rejection. Maybe you're confident that they will love and support you... but that it will forever change the nature and structure of a relationship you cherish. Maybe the idea of losing any or all of that renders you unable to make the decision.

Maybe some of the people you love the most in this world will see your previous inability to be authentic with them as a form of deception and will feel hurt and betrayed. Maybe they won't quite understand just how paralyzed you've been. Maybe they can't quite grasp that you were unable to acknowledge or accept who you were, and it was therefore absolutely impossible for you to admit it to anyone else.

> *Outside factors can influence you, but ultimately the locus of control is 100% inside you.*

Believing you don't have a choice to be exactly who you are renders you powerless to embrace authenticity. I understand this because it used to be my reality. Sure, the specific details may have been different, but I too felt pressured into a choice to be who the world wanted me to be, to do only what I was allowed and expected to do.

It's nothing personal. It's your reality. Your chosen reality. That's not a judgment, it's an observation. A neutral one. There's no shame in admitting that it was a choice. It was a choice that you felt pressured into, but it was a choice. The fear, guilt, shame, and doubt were overwhelming. They were too strong to overcome. The fear of the fallout was too great to choose authenticity. In choosing conformity you found safety. It was still a choice, your choice.

Like you, and countless others, I felt powerless and incapable of choosing to be myself, until something, or more accurately *someone,* came along and helped me find the courage to rebel.

That someone was my daughter Frankie. She was nine months old when I finally understood the cost of conformity and inauthenticity. Suddenly, there was something more terrifying than sharing the real me with the world. The realization that I was destined to teach this precious child that it was okay for her to be anything other than exactly who she is was heartbreaking. I didn't want her to feel as though any part of her was less than exceptional. I couldn't tolerate the thought of her being confined by the judgmental expectations of the world around her. I couldn't fathom a future in which she was limited by what the world would allow.

The degree to which I didn't want that for my daughter was palpable. I could feel it in my bones and to my core. Sure, I could tell Frankie all these things, but every word would be tainted with inauthenticity. It would be an exercise in hypocrisy rooted in my inability to do what I was trying so desperately to teach her.

There's a saying that perfectly describes this notion, and it's highly ineffective because it's absolute crap. "Do as I say, not as I do." In order to be the parent I desperately wanted to be, I needed to find the courage to rebel. I had to overcome the pressure to conform. I needed to come face to face with my fear of the fallout and emerge victorious. I did it for her. I did it for me. I did it for everyone in my life that I loved and, as I would come to learn, I did it for people I hadn't even met yet who desperately needed to see that something previously considered inconceivable was entirely possible.

6

COMING OUT

"Wanna fly, you got to give up the shit that weighs you down."

—*Toni Morrison*

I signed up for a personal development and leadership course that I had no business committing to. The world was still reeling from a global pandemic, and the live events industry (and our photography company's revenue) had been decimated by people's inability to gather. How then did I find myself investing a hefty sum for a program that would prove to be one of the best things that ever happened to me?

Late on a Friday afternoon I got a text message from my friend Jorge. He wanted me to consider signing up for a program that he really liked and so we hopped on a Zoom to chat about it. I know what you may be thinking, and yes, he had participated in the program personally, and no, he didn't receive a commission of any sort. We looked at the website together. To say there was not much information on the page would be an understatement. It only listed the title, the duration, and the investment. There were no details, no testimonials, no promised outcomes. Just some cheery whimsical photos, the dates, and the price. It wasn't cheap.

Candidly, I thought he was kidding. Was this a prank or a test just to see if he could get me to agree to something with virtually no details? I had no good reason to invest in a three-month immersive program – regardless of how much Jorge liked it. I mean, I absolutely had the time, but I certainly didn't have the money. Oh, and another thing... the program closed at 5:00 PM that day, so I had only ninety minutes to decide. Well, that made it pretty simple and easy. NO.

But Jorge didn't take that first no for an answer.

Let me add some backstory. At this point, although I had acknowledged and accepted that I was nonbinary, I was still figuring out what that meant for me. I was also on the fence about if, when, and how I wanted to share my gender identity with the world. I was out to Emily and my family and a few very close friends, but that was it. I had known Jorge for a few years. We had become close and he had proven himself to be someone I could trust; however, I wasn't ready to tell anyone else, and that included him.

Back to that Zoom call and my NO that Jorge wouldn't accept. I should probably tell you that he is caring, kind, and remarkably charming. Jorge smiled and said that he understood, and then he asked me to hear him out. Ironically, he wouldn't tell me about the program – which I would come to learn was by design.

He started by offering me his perspective on fear, because he could clearly see I was afraid. Afraid of the program. Afraid of the commitment. Afraid of the cost. Afraid of the outcome. Yeah, I was pretty much living in fear.

There is no such thing as being fearless.

He reassured me by saying that there is no such thing as being *fearless*. We are all subject to some measure of fear at all times. He went on to say that these fears are a lot like taking children on a roadtrip. You can't leave them behind, you can't put them in the trunk, and above all else, you can't let them drive. I laughed out loud at the comparison, imagining five-year-old Frankie behind the wheel of our Ford F-150 on a long, lonely stretch of Texas highway with Emily and I white-knuckling in the back seat.

Despite this clever analogy, I held steadfast to my no. Undeterred, Jorge then offered something even more personal and heartfelt – something the universe clearly knew I needed to hear. He shared with me that he genuinely believed in me, and he believed in this program. He was sure that if I signed up, it would change my life forever.

Well, damn. How could I say no to that?

Just like this... NO.

I think he knew I was half kidding, so he encouraged me to go talk to Emily. He and my wife weren't quite as close but they were friends, and he knew us well enough to know that our relationship was special, our bond strong, and that she would offer me sound advice and loving encouragement. He knew she would be candid and constructive and that I deeply valued her thoughts and opinions. So, off I went to seek Emily's counsel.

Upon telling her all about Jorge's ambush, Emily casually looked at me and said that if Jorge really thought I should do it, then I should do it.

Dammit, again. But what about the money?

Yeah, Emily rarely worries about finances when it comes to things like this. She reassured me, as she always does, that it's only money, and that we can always make more. It was at that moment I realized I was completely out of excuses.

> *I was completely out of excuses.*

Dammit, a third (and final) time. I remained reluctant but nevertheless called Jorge and told him I was in.

I was about halfway through the program when Jorge's prediction became reality. During a particularly emotional exercise at the end of an exceedingly long day, I was encouraged to decide what it was that I wanted. They weren't talking about passing fancies or silly superficial wishes. They intended to unearth my sincerest wants and my deepest desires. Initially I kind of rolled my eyes and struggled to take the exercise seriously. I quickly noticed my own skepticism and shut it down. I wanted, or more accurately *needed*, to get as much as I could out of this program based on my investment of time and money.

Before long, I offered up that I didn't want to be afraid anymore. The moment I spoke those words, I knew I was on to something. I was informed that I "kinda did it wrong." (Of course I did). I needed to decide what I *wanted to be* rather than what I *didn't want to be*. So, I went back to work and offered up the words that would change my life... just like Jorge thought.

"I want to be courageous."

The moments that followed are a bit of a blur. The world fell away and I suddenly experienced the full weight of forty-five years of fear, guilt, shame, and doubt that had led to denying who I was, ignoring what I wanted, and hiding from everyone I ever met. I knew in that moment that everything was about to change. I had lived a painfully inauthentic life for far too long. It was time for me to proudly acknowledge who I was, to embrace what I wanted, and to show the world the real me.

I offered up the words that would change my life...

"I want to be courageous."

The session ran particularly late that evening. We finally wrapped for the night just before midnight. I was in our office-slash-guestroom in the back of the house. Not having heard a peep out of Emily for quite some time, I figured she had already gone to bed. The moment the call ended, I made my way down the hall to find our room dark and the bed empty. Odds were, she'd fallen asleep on the couch, but there was a slight chance that she was still awake, so I raced quietly down the stairs.

I rounded the corner and there Emily was, awake on the couch, waiting to hear all about my day. She denied herself the much-needed sleep a mother deserves so she could be there for me when I was ready for her. The respect, love, and appreciation I have for her knows no bounds.

I was excited to share my bold new intention with her. I sat on the ottoman across from her like I had on that hot August day in the park four years earlier. I looked into her eyes, ready to share the next step in my journey.

Just as before, the only thing I could offer her in that moment were tears.

Emily gave me a knowing look and leaned in to hold me, prepared to ride out yet another wave of emotional overwhelm like she had countless times before. We breathed together deeply while I regained my composure. She gently loosened her embrace and waited for me to confirm that I was ready to do the same. I took one last deep breath, fully acknowledging how grateful I am to have her as my wife. I squeezed her tightly for just a moment before gently releasing our embrace.

She placed her hands on either side of my face and gave me a reassuring smile as she wiped a tear from my eye with her thumb. I smiled back so she knew it was okay to leave me just long enough to get me tissues and a glass of water.

I took a sip of water and, as I cleaned myself up, I told Emily all about how I was ready to proudly declare to the world that I was nonbinary. I could tell how excited she was as she grabbed my neck, pulling me in for another hug, almost spilling my water. She whispered how happy she was for me in a way that reminded us both that, despite our shared excitement, we needed to keep it down so we wouldn't wake Frankie.

She asked if I had any ideas on how I wanted to go about coming out. This question hit me as ironic for two reasons. First, I had no idea how I wanted to come out, and second, I hadn't really thought of it as "coming out." Nevertheless, that's exactly what I was about to do – come out, a previously inconceivable act of unconditional self-love that would empower me to live each day with unapologetic authenticity for the rest of my life.

The next day, my creative and talented wife designed a beautiful graphic of a fingerprint overlaid with the colors of the nonbinary flag that I could share with my pronouns (they/them) to tell the world that "This is me. I'm Don Mamone and I'm nonbinary."

Because life happens and details get in the way, I don't talk with Jorge as often as I would like to anymore, but I will always be grateful for him, and that he didn't take NO for an answer.

The idea of coming out is largely associated with the LGBTQIA2S+ community. As a member of an often mistreated, misunderstood, and marginalized community, I certainly understand why. More than most, we're convinced at a young age that there's something wrong with us. That we're broken. That it's not okay to be who we are. Many of us bend to the pressure. We disguise a piece of who we are, only later to find ourselves in the regrettable position of needing to come out.

Don't get me wrong. Coming out is a good thing. A wonderful thing. Something worth celebrating. With that being said, I long for a day when nobody will ever need to come out again, simply because we'll have managed to create a world in which everyone gets to be exactly who they are from the day they are born and for the entirety of their life.

I remain ever-hopeful that a day will come when you don't need to be courageous to be who you are. Unfortunately, we're not there yet and there's quite a bit of work to do before we are. The process of coming out isn't reserved exclusively for the LGBTQIA2S+ community. Everyone has a coming out story. There comes a moment in everyone's life when they feel something about who they are isn't okay... including you. Can you recall a time when you felt as though you needed to keep a part of you hidden so you wouldn't face the fallout? Coming out is the moment when your fear turns to courage, your doubt turns to certainty, and your shame turns to pride.

> *Coming out is a good thing... but I long for a day when nobody will ever need to come out again...*

The range of thoughts and feelings that introduce and reintroduce the fear of fallout is wide and varies in degree and severity. It can quite literally be about anything that is a part of you or your identity. For the members of the LGBTQIA2S+ community, it's going to have something to do with things like gender identity, gender expression, sexuality, or sexual orientation.

...Like the woman who knew she wasn't much interested in physical intimacy or sex, but was so ashamed she consistently betrayed who she was for her spouse's wants and needs. Until she proudly declared, "I am asexual!"

...Like the homosexual nonbinary artist who was married to a person of the opposite sex because they couldn't admit who they were to their family, because anything other than a cisgender heterosexual existence was strictly forbidden. Until she proudly declared, "I am a nonbinary lesbian!"

For others it can have to do with things like who they love, what they want to do for a living, or even how they want to show up in the world.

...Imagine the college student who doesn't want to bring their significant other home because of race, religion, or nationality, because they know it will be an issue with the people in their family. Until she proudly declared, "I am in love with him and we're engaged to be married."

...What about the strong, confident woman who's passionate about her position and the company? She's a natural leader but doesn't speak up for fear that she will be seen as overly emotional, hysterical, or worst of all, bitchy.

...What about the successful, powerful female immigrant who is about to take the stage to present her TEDx Talk? She is visibly shaken and shares her concern that she will be judged and her message disregarded because of where she was born and her Arabic accent.

...What about the sensitive and compassionate man who's under considerable pressure, feeling the stress of a new project and deadline? He's overwhelmed but doesn't dare process his emotions in the presence of his coworkers because that wouldn't be professional, so he retires to a far-off restroom and cries quietly in one of the stalls.

...What about the adolescent who is considering where to apply to college and what their major gets to be, only to be told they can only apply to certain schools because they must become a doctor or lawyer? It doesn't matter that they want to be a musician, writer, or artist. They will become what their parent(s) say they will be... "or else" ...the fallout.

Just think about all the people who feel compelled to alter or diminish who they are or how they show up, for fear of the fallout. They worry what other people will think of them or what will be said about them.

These examples perfectly illustrate how people frequently fold when they come face to face with the fallout. These stories are not hypothetical. I have served each of these people in recent years, working as their identity coach. I am happy to report that all of them are well on their way to unwavering self-acceptance, unconditional self-love, and unapologetic authenticity.

The catalyst that introduces the gut-wrenching decision between conformity and authenticity can happen at any time, with anyone, in any environment. There's no such thing as a life free from this scenario. You can, however, take proactive steps toward ensuring that facing these decisions is the exception rather than the rule. This allows you to choose who you are and what's right for you rather than the offer of belonging, acceptance, and approval from outside yourself.

The moment you realize you get to choose your true and authentic self before anyone and everything else is very special. That's the moment you accept that there's nothing enticing enough or valuable enough to sacrifice even the smallest bit of who you are. People who truly love you will never ask you to compromise who you are or what feels right for you.

The sooner you realize you don't need to listen to the opinions, expectations, and limitations of others, the better. The sooner you understand the rules you were convinced applied to you are totally irrelevant, the better. The sooner you appreciate that the only acceptance and approval that matters is your own, the better. The sooner you accept that you're in charge of where you belong, the better. When all these elements come together in your head and in your heart, you will notice a perfect storm brewing. The winds of change will be upon you.

There is no right way to come out.

There's no right way to come out. There's also no right time to come out. Coming out is a deeply personal choice. It gets to happen when and if you're ready. You get to come out in whatever way feels right to you. You get to come out at whatever time feels right to you. You get to take into consideration *everything* and *everyone* you need to feel safe.

It's equal parts frustrating and refreshing to know that there's no right way to come out. On one hand, you won't find yourself needlessly worrying that you're not doing it right. On the other, there's no neatly packaged process to follow that makes it simple and easy either.

This is what I like to refer to as a "Congratulations, I'm sorry" moment. If you're considering when, where, why, how, or to whom to come out, that's certainly something to celebrate. You deserve a hardy "Congratulations." The reality that you need to figure out when, where, why, how, and to whom you're going to come out is daunting, intimidating, and, at times, terrifying. You deserve an empathetic "I'm sorry." You're on the verge of learning that it's not always easy (I'm sorry). You are also about to understand and appreciate that *it's worth it* (Congratulations)*!*

Now that you understand that coming out is a deeply personal journey and that no two stories are alike, it's going to be easier for you to make sure nobody "shoulds" all over you. That includes you. You get to make the decisions and you get to navigate the process. "Should-ing" all over yourself is the worst. This is your journey. You're in charge of every aspect of it: the who, the when, the where, the why, and the how.

I've learned that everyone gets to do this in their own time, at their own pace, and in their own way. That means you get to start if and when you're ready. You get to go as fast or slow as you want. And you get to follow whatever path and process makes sense for you. These three guidelines ensure you will seek and find the safety you need to successfully navigate your journey to coming out.

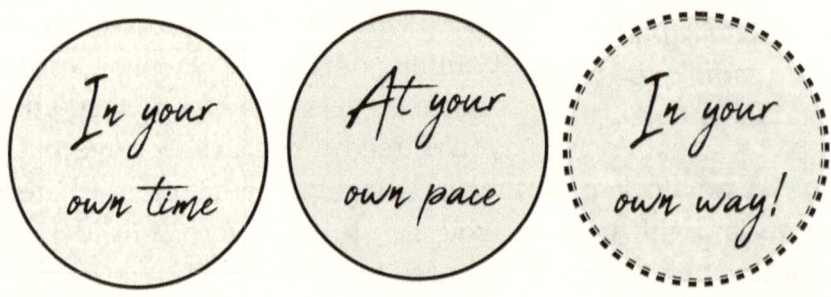

For me, letting people in began on that exceedingly hot and terrifying day with Emily in August of 2017. I suppose it continued with Frankie, although only technically so. At that point in my life, she was the only person with whom I was unconditionally authentic from the beginning. She was the first person to only ever know the real me. It didn't feel as though I was letting her in as much as it felt like I was just letting myself be.

I continued letting people in and began the process of coming out as I found the courage to face the fallout that was unique and specific to each of the relationships.

After Emily and Frankie, came my sister Gina. It was nearly three years to the day since I had let Emily in – August of 2020. Gina and I were talking about the upcoming holiday season and the fact that it was unlikely we would be able to be together as we had been nearly every other year for the entirety of our lives. Just another heartbreaking, gut-wrenching impact of the Covid-19 global pandemic. I was hoping I would have the opportunity to share my truth with her in person, but that seemed to be less and less likely as the year pressed on.

Looking back on it now, I think I may have been using the hope of holiday time together as a way to delay facing the fallout. Much like Emily, I was confident that Sissy would be loving, kind, and compassionate. The fallout I feared with her was different than with Emily. I mean, we were siblings who were incredibly close, so the likelihood that she would say she couldn't go on this journey was not really a concern. With Sissy, the fallout had more to do with the fact that I cherished the closeness I shared with her and her family. I was terrified that when I shared who I really was, it would forever change the nature, dynamic, and even the quality of our relationship.

> *What if my coming out created a gap or drove a wedge between us?*

What if she couldn't understand or accept the real me? What if my coming out created a gap or drove a wedge between us that meant we wouldn't be as close as before? What if our families would no longer share in our struggles and celebrate our successes? What if...?

Sissy and I FaceTime to get and give regular updates, guidance, and advice, although I'm confident I get more advice than I give. It was Friday. Sissy and I were chatting about the week when our conversation turned to the likelihood that we would spend the holidays apart. That being the case, I figured it was as good a time as any to let her in.

There was only one problem, I couldn't do it. Much like my conversation with Emily three years earlier, I became overwhelmed by emotion. So I told Sissy I had to go and we hung up, but not before we said the thing that had become a tradition among our family members.

"OK, love you. Bye."

Despite not having the courage to come out over the phone, I knew I wanted Sissy to know. I needed her to know. So I settled for the less than ideal, but much more manageable option. I texted her. Technology offered me the ability to put it out there no matter how emotionally overwhelmed I got. Conveniently, it has also allowed me to go back to those messages and reflect on the conversation so I can share the details with you.

In my first message I shared that, "I have been really struggling with my gender assignment, gender identity, and gender expression for a long time now."

One thing was beautifully clear... ...my coming out might just bring us closer together.

Her matter-of-fact response of "OK, and...?" was disarming and made me smile. This was such a "Sissy response."

I went on to explain in more detail what I was going through and how I felt.

Gina was just as kind and loving and compassionate as I'd anticipated. She was curious and supportive. She asked questions and offered advice. Some of her questions were softballs and others were 100 MPH fastballs right down the middle. Some advice was insightful whereas other was well-meaning but misguided.

Regardless, all of this was welcome and comforting because it was exactly the kind of conversation she and I have had countless times. I still had plenty to figure out, and we still had lots to discuss, but one thing was beautifully clear; I was certain my coming out would not create a gap or drive a wedge between us. I felt a glimmer of hope that it might just bring us closer together.

And it did.

7

INVISIBLE NO MORE

> "I am invisible, understand,
> simply because people refuse to see me."
>
> —*Ralph Ellison*

At the start of my speaking career, the topics I shared largely focused on business stuff – branding, marketing, lead generation, and sales conversion. I was committed to supporting entrepreneurs and career-focused professionals as they navigated the ups and downs of business by teaching them the ins and outs of what I'd learned over the past quarter-century.

In 2020, I submitted a presentation to speak at one of my favorite annual summer conferences. Because of Covid-19's stranglehold on the world, the event was canceled. The following spring, the organization reached out to tell me they were planning to safely and responsibly host their event in Las Vegas that August. They wanted to know if I was interested in being a speaker again that summer.

Of course I was. Or was I?

An unexpected hesitation washed over me as certainty gave way to doubt and confusion.

I had spoken at this conference numerous times. The audience was full of people I knew well. So why would I hesitate? Speaking is my jam; it was a conference that I knew, and an audience that I loved.

Then I realized, despite all that, things were different now. I was different now. Before accepting their invitation I would need to do some soul searching to figure out exactly what was going on. And I would have to figure it out quickly if I didn't want to miss out on the opportunity to do what I loved with people I adored.

At first, I thought my hesitation may have been rooted in insecurity. I had literally just come out. I shared with the world that I was nonbinary through emails, conversations, and social media. Maybe I was concerned that I would not be accepted based on my gender identity or expression.

It didn't really feel like that was the reason. I was more certain of who I was and more secure than ever before. In fact, I think I surprised myself. After a lifetime of caring too much what other people thought and desperately seeking their approval, I didn't much seem to care about any of that anymore. I finally understood that other people's opinions of me are none of my business. For the first time, I was prepared to be exactly who I was, regardless of where I went or who I was with. That included Las Vegas, on that stage and with that audience.

I was more certain of who I was, and more secure than ever before.

If my hesitation wasn't rooted in an insecurity about myself, the audience, or the environment, what was left? The content. Having admitted that things were different, that I was different, maybe it didn't sit well with me that the presentation topic was the same.

I focused my energy and attention on the details of my proposal. Rather than the traditional business stuff they were used to, I wanted to share my story and journey. I wanted to frame it in such a way that it would be relevant and interesting to the audience. I wanted to ensure it would be beneficial to both them and me. Then, it hit me. I could educate the audience on what gender is, what it isn't, how it's experienced, and how to create safer spaces for people living courageously outside the gender binary. Most people have little or no knowledge of, or experience with, gender fluidity and nonconformity. It was within my power to do something about that. I was prepared to honestly and vulnerably share my story from the stage. I was prepared to encourage them to challenge their belief systems. I was prepared to ask them to open their hearts and minds and create safer spaces for people like me. I was prepared to watch them learn something new and different. I was prepared to show them that different doesn't mean broken – for me and for them.

With a renewed focus and sense of purpose, I replied to the association. I let them know that I was excited to be a part of their conference again, but that I would like to submit a new topic for consideration. I gave them a brief description of what to expect.

They quickly replied that they were not only okay with the change, they were eager to hear more. So, I crafted the details, completed the submission form, held my breath, and clicked submit.

> *I knew that a rejection of my proposal would not be a rejection of me... but the two were hard to separate.*

My attention shifted from creation to concern. I immediately began to wonder about the outcome of this submission. I had put the new me, the real me, out there for "consideration." I knew that a rejection of my proposal would not be a rejection of me, but given the personal nature of the subject matter, the two were hard to separate.

Just a few weeks later I received word that my submission had been accepted, and they were looking forward to my session. As I read those words and processed what they meant, I once again noticed emotions creeping in. I didn't so much notice them as I was overwhelmed by them.

All the anticipation and worry gave way to relief, joy, excitement, and a host of other powerful emotions.

The one emotion missing? Hesitation.

I was about to boldly, confidently, and unapologetically show up as my authentic self. I finally understood that if someone, anyone, chose not to see me, that didn't mean I was invisible; it meant they were blind.

It was long past time for me to show up, but as you can imagine, it's kind of hard to do that if you're not certain who you are. When you can't even see yourself, there's no way for you to know how you want to show up, let alone how you want to be seen by others.

> *If someone chose not to see me, that didn't mean I was invisible; it meant they were blind.*

Throughout my life in hiding, I considered any number of things that I might be or could be. Each of them was something to be ashamed of because it was weird or different. Each one confirmed what I most feared; I was broken.

One of my earliest memories of what felt right was wearing that satin skirt. For a while, I emulated this sensation with clothes like an extra long t-shirt that felt like a dress, or shorts that could be worn like a skirt. Later I bought articles of clothing at thrift stores so I could wear them when I was alone. Anything that fit like and felt like traditionally feminine clothing felt right – just like it always had.

Everything about that felt right except needing to keep it a secret. For the longest time, I thought I was a cross dresser. It seemed simple enough, albeit still unacceptable to my adolescent brain. I liked to wear what people considered to be clothing designed for women, so that must mean that I was a cross dresser. I even tested that theory out on what is often considered a cross dresser's Christmas – Halloween.

It was my junior year of high school. One of my friends was throwing a party, so I needed to come up with a costume. I could have done any number of clever, fun, or scary costumes but there was one that stood out and piqued my interest. The idea that I could wear and do what felt right, without the overwhelming feelings of fear or shame, simply because it was Halloween, was irresistible.

I borrowed a denim mini-skirt, a black blouse, and two-inch black kitten heels. Gina did my makeup and styled my hair, although I ended up wearing a black wide brim hat since my haircut was high and tight.

The entire evening was amazing. I never wanted it to end. But I knew it would. The idea that I would ever be able to experience this open, free, authentic feeling the other 364 days of the year was nestled between inconceivable and impossible.

Eventually, I started to understand that I was not a cross dresser. It was more than that for me. Cross dressing is something a person does; this was about who I am. At first I was disappointed. I had once again discovered something I wasn't. It didn't feel as though I was any closer to discovering my true self. In actuality, learning who you are not is just as helpful as learning who you are. Each trait, characteristic, core value, and belief you eliminate gets you one step closer to understanding who you are.

> *Learning who you are not is just as helpful as learning who you are.*

I abandoned the label of cross dresser and all the others I'd considered. None of them were suitable. The lone exception was one that always seemed to fit. It was the label I was unable to escape – broken.

In the four years since I'd let Emily in, the prevailing theme in my life was exploration. Sitting on that picnic table in the park, I still had no idea who I really was or what I really wanted. I've come to accept that even when we do know what we want, it's still common to not have the language to express it to others.

It was time for me to do a different kind of work. It was time to dig deep and figure myself out. It was time to explore who I might be, to figure out who I was and who I wanted to become.

I started by voraciously consuming content of all kinds from a variety of reputable sources. I read articles in medical journals and abstracts from contemporary scientific and medical research. I watched videos from gender scholars, doctors, and mental health professionals. I read books and articles chronicling personal stories from members of the trans community. I watched documentaries, movies, and television shows that felt relatable to my journey.

> *Even when we do know what we want, it's still common to not have the language to express it to others.*

I relentlessly devoured all things gender and gender adjacent. Much like the notion of being a cross dresser, I started by uncovering who I *wasn't* as much as I worked toward figuring out who I was and who I wanted to become.

I pretty much knew that I wasn't cisgender. I realized my sex assigned at birth didn't align with my gender identity. Beyond that, I wasn't certain of much else. I toyed with the notion that I was a transgender female. That didn't quite feel authentic but I reserved the right to take my time and change my mind along the way. I knew that the further I ventured past what was expected of me and what I'd been allowed to do, the harder and more complicated the journey. My commitment to authenticity meant limitless potential and profound opportunity.

The fallout never goes away entirely. I could beat it back and take away its power, but it's always out there. The fallout is lurking, waiting for an opportunity to plant a "what if" in your mind that sends you running for shelter.

Emily told me she knew I was her person two weeks after we met. She said that we were in this for life… and yet, there was still a "what if" rattling around in my brain. Despite consistently reassuring me that she was my lobster (because according to Phoebe from *Friends,* lobsters mate for life), I still worried that something I discovered could be a bridge too far for her, and she would decide that despite her best efforts and intentions this was no longer something she could handle and a journey she couldn't go on with me.

It felt like every moment, every thought, every choice, and every decision was ridiculously complicated and fraught with both hope and dread. That was my new reality. A series of "Congratulations, I'm sorry" moments.

For the first time, maybe ever, it wasn't so much about the fear as it was about the fragility. Fear is about what we can't do, something that we can't face, an obstacle we can't overcome, or a barrier we can't break through. Fragility, on the other hand, is about what's expected of us, what we're not allowed to do, and what we're not supposed to do. Suddenly, I wasn't afraid of the fallout. I was discouraged by how fragile I felt as I prepared to stand up and act in defiance of a rigid and judgmental society.

Apparently, I would no longer allow myself to be limited by the fear of possible fallout… only to be overwhelmed by unlimited potential.

I decided I could tame that sense of overwhelm by putting on the most fabulous and beautiful pair of metaphorical blinders you've ever seen. I could completely ignore all that nonsense if I just focused all my effort and attention on the one thing that mattered. I would doggedly seek anything and everything that felt right to me. I unequivocally knew what that felt like. I would fully embrace those feelings and completely ignore all the noise and distractions.

The beauty of my new plan was rooted in its simplicity. It wasn't always easy but it was always simple. I could reflect on any thought that entered my mind, make any choice I wanted, and be confident in every decision I made, with the only rule being that I would relentlessly search my feelings.

> *Just because something felt uncomfortable, didn't mean it was wrong or inauthentic.*

Like a proper Jedi, I quickly learned that I would need to be patient. Just because something felt uncomfortable didn't mean it was wrong or inauthentic. Something that was unacceptable for the entirety of my life would certainly feel odd or unnatural.

I set out to carefully sort through my feelings to determine who I was and who I wasn't. It was hard, intricate work, because some of the things that were absolutely right for me were cleverly disguised as things I was not allowed to be or do.

I routinely reminded myself that I was allowed to do and be anything I wanted to do or be. I literally repeated this affirmation in my head. I spoke it aloud. I even wrote it down frequently when doubt would stop by for a visit, trying to derail my efforts and erode my confidence.

Before I tell you more about what I discovered about myself, it's important for me to give you a crash course on gender. By learning a bit about what I now know, you'll better understand my journey. You'll be prepared to see me as I am. You'll be able (and hopefully willing) to expand your system to accommodate others rather than expecting them to accommodate your system. In doing all this, I suspect you'll be emboldened to demand the same for yourself.

Gender

The idea of gender has been oversimplified and misunderstood for a very long time. Most people's understanding of gender is reduced to either "girl" or "boy" based entirely on anatomy. They believe that an individual's gender is dictated by the genitals they have at birth.

For much of my life, I was under this same impression. That belief contributed considerably to feeling broken. If the only acceptable option was "girl" or "boy," then feeling as though I was both must be unnatural and unacceptable, right?

Wrong.

The human tapestry of identity and gender is too emotionally intricate and beautifully complex to restrict to just this or that. We now know that the only thing we learn about the precious bundles of joy being brought into the world is their sex assigned at birth. A person's gender and their sex assigned at birth are not the same thing. That may be hard for some people to wrap their heads around, but that doesn't make it any less true.

A person's gender consists of four base elements: gender identity, gender expression, attraction, and biological sex. Here's a quick introduction to each of these elements.

- Gender Identity – Who you know yourself to be in your head and your heart.

- Gender Expression – How you choose to share who you are with the world.

- Attraction – Who you are attracted to physically, emotionally, romantically, and psychologically.

- Biological Sex – Your anatomical make-up, including your genitals, chromosomal makeup, hormones, your primary and secondary sex characteristics, and more.

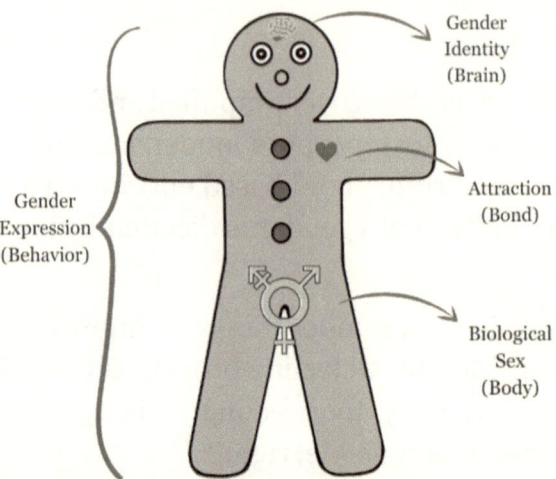

Each of these elements[2] is interrelated but none of them are interdependent. They can impact and affect one another but they can also change and evolve independently. None of these elements dictate what the others are or will be. A person's gender is a unique combination of these four elements. Each is beautiful and all are valid and deserving of kindness and respect.

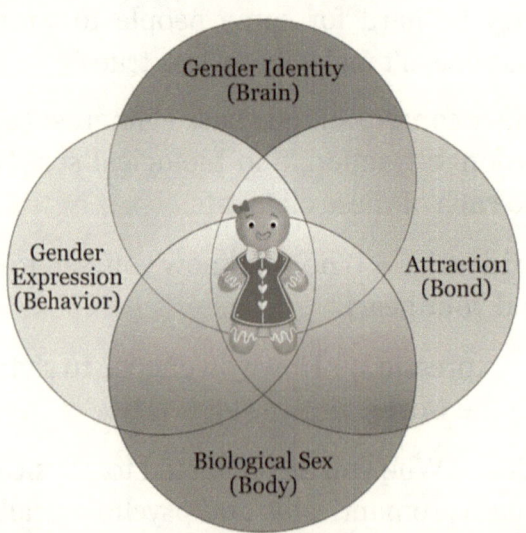

I learned quite a bit about gender in the four years between letting Emily in and coming out. I also learned quite a bit about myself by

---

[2] Genderbread Person, created and uncopyrighted 2017 by Sam Killermann, adapted by the author.

listening as I learned. I paid particularly close attention to how I reacted and how I felt as I gained knowledge and challenged my belief system.

At times, my reactions, thoughts, and feelings were not as I would have hoped. They were not in alignment with my commitment to authenticity. They were rooted in the conventional and restrictive foundations I had been taught – rules I followed far too long.

That made sense, since I was working against muscle memory that had been trained over the entirety of my life. My reactions, thoughts, and feelings were often automatic. Literally, I didn't even have the time to sift, sort, or process. It was instantaneous. I couldn't help myself. What I could do was recognize when it was happening and ensure these responses never influenced my words or actions. I could listen intently to my heart. It would guide me by whispering who I was and how I wanted to show up. These reactions, thoughts, and feelings were largely aligned with my foundations and would live only inside me. That would afford me the time I needed to keenly identify and reject them as unwanted and unnecessary.

The filters through which I see and operate in the world are now an authentic reflection of me.

Curious, not judgmental

One of the character traits I recognized as hardwired in my brain because of my foundations is the habit of being judgmental. I never liked this about myself. For years I've said that I want to be less judgmental. I appreciate and envy a lack of judgment in others, but despite my best effort and considerable determination, I've never been able to shake it. That's because it's foundational. It was engrained in me before I had a voice and a choice.

What I have been able to change is what I do with that judgment once it's already in my head.

I never allow it to travel to my heart, mouth, or body. I see the world through filters of love, acceptance, and curiosity. These are also the lenses through which I want the world to see me. I have no desire to judge others and I most certainly don't want to be judged. Despite involuntary judgmental thoughts, my words and actions are those of a loving, accepting, and curious person.

You are the sum total of your thoughts, words, and actions. Sometimes your outdated foundational elements remind you of who you don't want to be and how you don't want to act or react. That's how you filter out unwanted habits and behaviors. That's how you become the aspirational version of yourself. That's how you become immensely proud of how far you've come, what you've accomplished, and who you are. With deliberate practice you are not only capable of change, but you also have the potential to truly shine.

Unapologetic authenticity is the bold, courageous extension of "letting people in" and "coming out." It's an unwavering commitment to being exactly who you are, everywhere you go, no matter who you're with. Your intention is to never hide or deny who you are, so that you never have to let someone in or come out to anyone ever again.

The shame you once let drive you into hiding is replaced with a pride that fosters unconditional self-love.

As you disentangle who you pretended to be from who you truly are, you become increasingly content and comfortable. You develop a confidence regarding not only who you are but also how you expect the world to see you. You find the courage to stand up for how you want to be treated. The shame you once let drive you into hiding is replaced with a pride that fosters unconditional self-love and audacious authenticity.

You get to be loved *because* of who you are, rather than in spite of it.

"I am"

There are a great many words in the English language, but no two are more powerful than "I am..." They're the start of a declarative statement or affirmation about who you are.

You might declare, "I am nonbinary." Or you might affirm "I am courageous." Statements and affirmations both represent something you're ready to share with the world. They are proof of your confidence, courage, and pride. They play a pivotal role in letting people in, coming out, and being seen. They also affirm your identity. "I am" statements indicate to the world how you see yourself and how you expect to be seen by others.

You don't need to look outside yourself for validation or confirmation of your "I am" statements. They are true and accurate because you say they are, and you are the resident expert on you. Other people's thoughts, judgments, opinions, or criticisms of you are irrelevant.

The acts of letting people in, coming out, and being visible do not mean you must offer full and complete disclosure of everything you are, everything you're thinking, or everything you have planned. This is your journey. In the beginning – this most fragile time – choose someone you feel safe with, who will respect your process and pace. Remember, you get to do this in your own time, at your own pace, and in your own way. If you find yourself feeling rushed, judged, or compelled by those you have chosen, it's likely time to consider choosing someone else. If this person isn't offering empathy, compassion, or understanding, they are likely making the situation about them rather than you. It's definitely time to reconsider who you invite into your inner circle.

> *Coming out doesn't mean you must offer full and complete disclosure of everything.*

Secret vs. private

There is an essential and significant difference between keeping a secret and being private. This difference centers around choice. You feel compelled to keep a secret, whereas you choose to keep something private. Unapologetic authenticity and privacy are not mutually exclusive. They can exist happily in harmony. I choose to live an out, proud, and publicly visible life in the hope that I can serve as an inspiration to others while still choosing to keep plenty of things private.

There is empowerment in choosing to keep something private. There is fragility in feeling forced to keep a secret. I was convinced that there was something about me that wasn't okay. Something that was unacceptable. Something wrong. Something *broken*. I was convinced I needed to keep my secret because if anyone found out how different I was, the fallout would be devastating.

Keeping that secret for all those years was the main reason I felt broken. Keeping that secret was why I cried myself to sleep countless nights. Keeping that secret was the reason I hoped, wished, and prayed I could just be normal. Laying alone in my childhood bed, I believed my life would all be better if I could just figure out how to fix what was broken so I wouldn't be forced to keep this secret anymore.

Now that I've freed myself of this weight, my life is infinitely better. Being normal wasn't the way out from under its crushing burden. Radical self-acceptance is the way. Unconditional self-love is the way. Unapologetic authenticity is the way. Knowing that you are valid, that you matter, and that you are enough is the way. Understanding that there's nothing to fix about you – because different doesn't mean broken – was, is, and always will be the way.

8

THE WINDFALL

> "Great things are not accomplished by those who yield to trends and fads and popular opinion."
>
> —*Jack Kerouac*

Emily is a watcher and a listener, which is really convenient since she is a photographer and musician. She routinely uses what she sees and hears as motivation for what she captures and creates. She draws on her experiences to write lyrics and compose music that listeners can not only relate to but feel to their very core. She creates deeply personal musical and photographic experiences that impact both concert audiences and art aficionados. All that being said, she's not so keen on the spoken word. We often say that in our family, I am the orator and Emily is the interjector.

On anniversaries and other special occasions (and frequently on a random Tuesday) I will say and write beautiful, romantic things to my wife. I want her to know just how much I love her. I want her to know that I appreciate her unconditional love and support. I want her to know that I am grateful for her, every minute of every day. I want her to know that I wish I could turn back the clock and meet her sooner so I could love her longer.

As she reads or listens to my words, she is truly taking them in and is emotionally moved by them. Then she typically looks me deep in my eyes, and with all the love in her heart and all the sincerity she can muster, she says, "Aww. Me too, babe." Or, simply says with a smile, "Ditto."

I can't help but smile when I think about it, because it's now a running joke between us. Her lack of comfort with the spoken word is just one more thing about her that I cherish and adore. I find it endearing to watch her work to formulate her feelings into words while I patiently wait to fully receive whatever it is that she has to offer. There are times when, in her determination to share her love and insight, she doesn't struggle in the least. She has something momentous to say and, damn it, she says it. It's in these moments that I am often overcome with emotion and reduced to a puddle of tears.

Before we were a family, we were a couple. Before we were a couple, we were individuals.

One of these special interactions happened on a typical date night. Emily and I have always honored the building blocks of our relationship. Before we were a family we were a couple, and before we were a couple we were individuals. We respect all of these elements in relatively equal measure. We live our life as a family, we create opportunities to honor our relationship as a couple, and we respect one another as individuals – even eight-year-old Frankie.

Back to date night. It was Saturday and we were invited to an event downtown. We were overdue for some couple time so I scheduled Frankie's favorite babysitter, Liam, and told our daughter all about our plan of action (POA) for the evening. Frankie loves a good POA because it helps her understand what to expect and lets her prepare for what's to come. When Liam comes over, she typically wants to make something to give to him. She has also gotten in the habit of creating her own little POA for the two of them.

The Windfall

One of my favorite things about date nights happens before we even leave our house. The time Emily and I spend getting ready together is just as special as our night out. It doesn't matter where we're going, what we're doing, or who we're going to be with, I love getting ready with Emily. Each time she asks me what I'm planning to wear and offers her advice on my outfit and accessories, I feel seen. Every time we put on our makeup together, I feel accepted. Every time she tells me how beautiful I look, I feel wanted. Every time she proudly takes my hand as we walk to wherever we're headed, I feel loved.

> *One of my favorite things about date night is the "getting ready."*

I don't recall what we decided to wear or where we were headed that particular date night. I'm also not certain what time of year it was, although I seem to think it may have been the fall or maybe even the holiday season. I'm not even sure what we were talking about before Emily looked over at me and said that she had something really important she wanted to tell me.

At that moment I heard the sound of a needle scratching across a vinyl record. When Emily has something she wants to share with me, everything else takes a backseat to what she's about to say. Suddenly, our typical date night was anything but. I can't recall any of the other particulars about that evening, but the next moment is burned into my memory. We were on the Dallas North Tollway headed downtown. Emily was driving and I was riding shotgun, which was a good thing since I was about to be overcome with emotion... again.

Emily started talking about our relationship. She told me that she loved me for many reasons. She loved me because I was kind, that I cared a great deal for everyone in my life, and that I was driven and motivated to chase my dreams and support others in achieving theirs. She even admitted to loving me for the big orange cuddly tabby cat that I had when we first met. She loved that I let

Gizmo cuddle on my lap for as long as she wanted, routinely making me late for important things like going to work and picking up Emily for dates. To sum it all up, she said she loved that I was a great person with a beautiful soul and a wonderful heart.

I'm sure she could tell that I was on the verge of tears. I was also at a loss for words, which was just fine because she wasn't quite through.

Emily wanted me to know all of these wonderful things because, after I "let her in," she witnessed me become a better spouse and a better parent. She was the first person to ever see the real me and what she saw as I came out was a better photographer, a better speaker, a better coach, and a better writer. A better everything.

She shared that she was not alone in this belief. She'd had conversations with my sister who agreed I was a better sibling, and she'd spoken with our friends who said I was a better friend.

> *After I "let her in," she witnessed me become a better spouse, a better parent... a better everything.*

I leaned my head back and fanned my face, reminding Emily that she's not supposed to make me cry when I'm wearing makeup. This little joke was just enough to usher forth a laugh and keep the tears right where they were, at the edge of streaming down my face.

I thanked Emily for her beautiful words and meaningful compliments. She was no longer alongside me on my journey. She had pulled ahead and was leading me by seeing and accepting things that I hadn't yet been willing or able to notice. She knew that being my authentic self had allowed me to find all the best parts of me so I could share them with the world. She used her perfectly curated words to share a keen observation of, and loving appreciation for, the real me.

The Windfall

Just as I had hoped, the benefits of coming out and living authentically exceeded the losses. In that moment I understood that "the windfall" was far greater than "the fallout."

You are already familiar with "the fallout." It's the collection of perceived negative consequences that you fear will befall you, if and when you abandon conformity and fight for authenticity.

"The windfall," on the other hand, is the collection of positive outcomes that you hope will await you, if and when you abandon conformity and fight for authenticity.

I chose to call this collection of good tidings "the windfall" because of how elusive it tends to be. The positive outcomes play hard-to-get. I mean, it's hard to imagine anything good coming out of something you've been intimidated by and afraid of for so long. We're much more familiar with the risk of the fallout than the reward of the windfall.

> *We're much more familiar with the risk of the fallout than the reward of the windfall.*

The voices inside your head that run on repeat are a constant reminder of all the terrible things that could happen if you leave the safety of your fallout shelter. Those voices have you convinced that there are no positive outcomes to be had. They whisper, or shout, that there is no windfall, only the fallout.

That's an absolute lie. You may doubt the existence of "the windfall," but that doesn't make it any less real. I am going to pull back the curtain and expose the windfall for what it really is – an absolute certainty. Not a possibility, not a probability… a certainty. I realize this may be hard to accept since it's counter to elements of your foundation and lived experience. Nevertheless I am prepared to encourage and reassure you so you too can summon the courage to leave that fallout shelter for good.

I realize how incredibly fortunate I am. I also acknowledge my considerable privilege. Many of the negative consequences I expected as a part of the fallout were not as tragic as I had imagined or were altogether nonexistent. The positive outcomes, on the other hand, were numerous and beyond my wildest imagination. With that being said, I am not special in this regard. There is nothing about my coming out story that predisposed me to a lesser fallout or a greater windfall than anyone else – including you.

This is the formula. You dramatically overestimate the fallout and your ability to bear it. You tragically underestimate the windfall and the positive impact it will have on you, your life, and the people you love.

That is just the way it is when you've been hiding, denying, and avoiding your way through life. I don't necessarily need you to believe that this is true based on my experience alone. I just need you to acknowledge that it's possible. When you are finally ready to abandon conformity and embrace authenticity, I need for you to find and foster an enduring faith in your strength and in this process.

Still reluctant and feeling skeptical? That's perfectly okay. I was too. I was terrified. On that hot August day in the park with Emily, I expected total devastation, at least in the short term. Deep down I hoped there would be a glimmer of hope on the horizon, but there was no evidence of it in that moment. The same may be true for you when you first emerge from your shelter, but I assure you the windfall awaits you on the other side.

I am painting a pretty picture but at the same time it's important to manage your expectations. You will suffer from negative consequences and benefit from positive outcomes. There is no pattern and no predicting what comes next. The two don't always come together and they rarely come in equal measure. Sometimes the journey seems more tolerable; other times it seems untenable. Unbelievable highs are followed by unbearable lows. The negative consequences and positive outcomes may cancel each other out, leaving you feeling apathetic, almost numb. In each of these scenarios, and countless others, hold on to your faith. Eventually and inevitably, the windfall crushes the fallout.

Since the windfall is a cheeky little monkey that doesn't readily flaunt itself, here are some of the ways it's likely to show up in your life.

Right after I let Emily in, you may be thinking that the windfall was her positive response, and you would be half right. Her unconditional love and acceptance clearly go in the windfall column. But I wouldn't describe that as my first windfall. As soon as I finally shared the words, a tremendous weight lifted and I was filled with an overpowering sense of relief. It was done; I did the hardest thing I'd ever attempted, and I was still standing. I was still there, with her, in that park, on that hot day, ready to face whatever was next. No matter what happened from that moment on, I would never have to go back to the time when I was keeping this secret from her.

Repression and suppression are cruel masters to serve.

Repression and suppression are cruel masters to serve. You work hard and they demand quite the price. Suddenly, all the energy and effort I had spent worrying about and keeping my secret were now free to be spent on more positive and productive things. All the guilt and shame were gone. I felt lighter, freer. I could breathe again.

If I think back over the years when I was too scared and intimidated to acknowledge and accept the real me, I don't recall coming out being a consideration. It's not as though I'd thought through all my options, or considered all the outcomes and then decided I would remain in hiding. Coming out was never an option so there was no reason to waste my time thinking about it.

There was also no reason for me to consider how my life might be better if I did come out. I believed that the life that I was living was the only life I would ever live. The inauthentic and fragmented version of me that I manufactured was the only me I would ever be. There was no path to authenticity and, even if there was, I couldn't see it. And, even if I could see it, I didn't have the strength and courage to move from where I was. I was blinded and paralyzed by the fear of the fallout.

You can't control how the people in your life will respond to your authentic identity. You can hope for the best, but you get to prepare for the worst. One of the most challenging acknowledgments is that even if the outcome is the realization of your worst fear, it's still worth it. Nothing is worth living your life as something you're not. When I first let Emily in, I really had no idea what she would say, or how she would react, or what it would mean for us as a couple. In that terrifying, vulnerable moment I went "all in," which meant losing it all was a very real possibility. Not knowing how she would respond, I needed to be prepared to go on without her. I was immensely relieved when Emily once again chose me. I was incredibly grateful that Emily promised I was her person and she would love me forever. I was overjoyed when Emily committed to continuing on this journey with me.

There were people in my life who loved and accepted me unconditionally, just like Emily – the windfall. There were also some who did not, and many of those people are no longer a part of my life – the fallout.

Your authenticity is like a bright beacon on a moonless night. People far and wide are going to see it. Some are going to be attracted to your light and others are going to be repelled by it. Consider those who draw near to be your people and a part of your windfall. In contrast, those who are repelled by your bright light are not your people and are not willing to do what it takes to be invited over to your side of that chalk line that represents the boundary set to protect yourself.

Interestingly, some of the people I was certain would be attracted to my light pulled away, and those I most expected to recoil raced to be at my side. Go figure. The moral of the story here is that people may come and people may go, but the most important person to consider is *you*.

Your windfall is really good at hiding in plain sight. You're going to be out there just living your best, most authentic life, not even realizing that many of the positive outcomes you experience in the future are a part of your windfall.

> *People may come, and people may go, but the most important person to consider is YOU.*

I can't tell you specifically what your negative consequences or positive outcomes will be, because I'm not you. Your journey is your own and entirely unique. This part of your story has yet to be written, and I don't have a crystal ball through which I can predict the future. What I do have is considerable experience and an abundance of confidence when I say that many, if not most, of these potential positive outcomes are possible for you.

...You will no longer have that secret simmering just below the surface, ready to boil over at any moment.

...You will no longer be hiding or denying things that are core to your identity.

...You will have unburdened yourself of that fear, guilt, shame, and doubt that was weighing you down and holding you back.

...You are going to identify and welcome the people who are prepared to accept and love you because of who you are, while rejecting those people who don't.

...Your increased clarity, confidence, and focus are going to help you understand what you want.

...You are going to be encouraged to pursue more and achieve greater.

...Your newfound joy, contentment, and strength will have a positive impact on your personal relationships and interpersonal communication.

...You are going to notice an increase in patience and understanding.

...You will find yourself leading with compassion and empathy.

...In seeing and accepting yourself, you will more easily see and accept others.

All of these positive outcomes are possible. But I've saved the best for last. I can all but guarantee that everyone who embraces unwavering self-acceptance, unconditional love, and unapologetic authenticity will experience this last one.

...You're about to discover and put to work in your life an incredible feeling of freedom that's beyond your wildest imagination... a freedom from the fear of the fallout, and the freedom to find your way to the windfall.

9

BECOMING

*"We delight in the beauty of the butterfly,
but rarely admit the changes it has gone through
to achieve that beauty."*

—Maya Angelou

I started to appreciate coffee for the same reason I started to appreciate many of the things I grew to love – my Italian family.

The settings of some of my fondest memories include various kitchens and dining rooms from childhood. That little modular home that my grandparents opened to us all those years ago had what one could only describe as modest proportions. The cooking space had everything a kitchen needed and not much else. There wasn't a ton of cabinets. The refrigerator wasn't very large, and the counter was just big enough for Nunnie to get done what she needed to do – feed a house full of people.

The things you would always find in abundance were flavors, aromas, and love. Feeding us (or more accurately, over-feeding us) was Nunnie's love language.

Meals routinely had many courses. First the salads, meats, and cheeses. Next the pasta dishes. Then came the main entrees including chicken, beef, and seafood. And, last, just when you felt as though you couldn't eat another bite, a lavish display of desserts and coffee were delivered to the table. My appreciation started with the sweet smell of coffee because I was too young to drink it. I'm fairly certain, however, that I was drinking coffee before most of my fellow American kids. I kind of feel like the Italians put coffee in baby bottles, but maybe that's just my imagination.

Similarly, Emily appreciated coffee pretty early in life, but for a very different reason. It wasn't unusual for her family to attend church services all day Sunday and church events on Wednesday. Dinner with the congregation always followed. They didn't have much at those events but they always had coffee, so that's what she drank. Services and coffee. Bible study and coffee. Choir practice and coffee. Emily left the church but kept the coffee.

Despite having different introductions to our favorite caffeine delivery system, Emily and I both still love coffee. Every morning we brew a fresh pot and start our day with a cup in our family room or, if weather permits, on our patio.

We don't always buy a particular brand. We don't grind our own beans fresh. We do, however, make it a little lavish by adding a teaspoon of raw sugar and some warm almond milk frothed to perfection. I suppose you can say our daily ritual is a tad bit fancy. It's clear that we love the coffee, but I know Emily would agree that our morning ritual is about more than the beverage. It's also about the time. It's about the conversation. It's about the connection. Every morning, the two of us start our day intentionally and with each other. We bond over coffee.

In our seventeen years together and fifteen years married, we've experienced the requisite ups and downs. We've celebrated good times and survived not so good times. In recent years, Emily supported me as I faced the fear of the fallout. She saw, accepted, and loved me unconditionally and without hesitation long before I ever could. She patiently waited until I was confident and comfortable enough to show myself to the world so I would no longer be invisible. She helped me understand that there was a windfall that would far outweigh the fallout.

The journey was long and so were the conversations. They didn't all take place in the morning over a freshly brewed cup of coffee but some of them did. And many started because of a simple question that Emily got in the habit of asking. "How are you feeling today?"

My responses varied from day to day, even moment to moment. There were times when I felt content, relieved, enthusiastic, and even optimistic. Mostly though, I was uncomfortable. Physically, emotionally, mentally – uncomfortable. Oh, and I was tired, too. I was uncomfortable and I was tired.

The discomfort and exhaustion were from consistently swimming upstream. I routinely did things that were counterintuitive and not at all what I was accustomed to. Everything was different than before (in all the best ways), but that didn't mean that my day-to-day existence wasn't challenging.

It was unrealistic to think that everything would magically be all good right away.

It was unrealistic to think that everything would magically be all good right away. It was unfair to think I wouldn't have considerable trouble with the radical transition from confinement to freedom. I figured there was still work to be done and knew there would continue to be ups and downs, but I'd also hoped that after all the emotional effort and turmoil to get where I was, the universe would cut me some slack.

Hope be damned. I had come so far and yet I couldn't help but feel as though things were actually harder and more complicated than before. Salt, meet wound. All that work. All that pain. All that heartache. All for nothing? That's how it felt.

It sounds dramatic and desperate because that's exactly how it felt. Turns out, I hadn't done a particularly good job of setting and managing my expectations. Which isn't altogether surprising since this was the first time I'd been through anything like this.

Emily's ability to affirm who I was created an unquestionably safe space for me. It was something I had never experienced before. When she said I was "her person," that she would love me forever, and that she wanted to go on this journey with me, I believed her. I could be, say, and do anything that felt right for me in the presence of another person for the first time in my life.

It was during one of our more emotional morning conversations that I told her through a fresh batch of tears how terrified I was to "be me." Sure, I had come out, spoken publicly about gender identity, and even started to experiment with my gender expression, but I was beginning to realize that despite all that, lingering feelings of intimidation and nervousness remained. I was quickly learning that it's one thing to admit to it, another thing to commit to it, and something else entirely to say, do, and be it.

It's one thing to admit... another to commit... and something else entirely to say, do, and be it.

Emily accepted and loved me, unconditionally, but I knew that not everybody would. The fear of fallout was once again looming, casting a long dark shadow over my newly minted authentic existence.

Emily looked at me with empathy, compassion, and understanding. She set down her mug before scootching closer to me on the couch. She wrapped her arms around me and squeezed me tight. I continued to give in to the emotional overwhelm, feeling safe in her embrace.

She pulled back but only far enough to catch my eye before she went to work on me. Emily started by telling me how much she loved me and our life together. She said she always knew that I was an amazing person and that I was getting better by the day as I discovered and embraced my authentic self. Then she went to work on the world. She said that if someone was unwilling to accept and love me for who I am, then maybe they weren't worth my time and effort. She said that there are always going to be skeptics and haters in the world and that they were ignorant and irrelevant. She reminded me that this is serious. This is my life. I get to set the boundaries. I get to make the rules. Those that don't like them, don't get to play.

I finally realized the reality Emily created for me would serve as the model for my entire life. Our existence together represented what I would now demand from the rest of the world. I would accept nothing less than unconditional acceptance and love from anyone and everyone who wanted to be a part of my life. Yet another beautiful lesson that originated with Emily.

Admittedly, "uncomfortable" and "tired" were a refreshing change of pace. They were quite a bit better than the fear, guilt, shame, and doubt that I was used to. Turns out the unwavering sense of freedom I'd quested for all my life was finally at my disposal, but sat somewhere on a spectrum between fairly complicated and completely overwhelming. I found myself trying to take a sip from a fire hose at full pressure. Try as I might to moderate my intake to get a refreshing sip, I was getting hammered. Soaked, I would end up embarrassed by the spectacle I just created for others to witness. Or would I?

> *"Uncomfortable" and "tired" were a refreshing change from the fear, guilt, shame, and doubt that I was used to.*

I'm certain that the me I used to be would absolutely stress about the spectacle. I would be concerned with how I looked, what others would think, what they would say, and how they would treat me. I would of course be worried about how all of those things would affect Emily and Frankie, too. That level of worry tends to stick with you, so the new me was a lot like the old me in that regard. But not for long.

I knew that the commitment I made to unapologetic authenticity would create a world in which I would no longer be concerned with such trivial things as other people's thoughts, words, and actions. I had this vision that my coming out would create nothing but fallout for both Emily and Frankie... but instead it brought an unexpected windfall. I would focus my attention and efforts on being exactly who I am, as well as doing what I wanted and what felt right.

All I needed to do was figure out who I am.

Becoming

Becoming who you are isn't about *creating* who you are. It's about *accepting* who you are.

I'd like to be able to say that what other people think, say, and do in response to who you are doesn't matter, but that's rarely true. In an ideal world, other people's opinions would be irrelevant and would have exactly zero impact on you and your identity. Sadly, that's not the reality.

We don't live in an ideal world. Other people's opinions and expectations probably have a considerable impact. They contribute to the fear of the fallout. They cause us to question who we are, what we're allowed to be, and what we're allowed to do. They destroy our confidence and strip us of our courage.

We wind up creating a version of ourselves that complies with the demands of others rather than creating an authentic representation that celebrates who we are. There's no judgment in that observation. It's incredibly common for people to choose conformity in order to feel safe.

Becoming is an act of defiance. It's the start of the rebellious process through which you come to understand that you

> *"Becoming" is an act of defiance.*

make the rules. As a rebel, you accept that you're the only person whose approval and acceptance you require. *Becoming* means rejecting the conformity and the safety you're used to in search of the authenticity you now crave. *Becoming* means separating and disentangling who you've pretended to be from who you really are. *Becoming* means abandoning the manufactured version of you the world wanted and needed. It means destroying who you created so the world could incorrectly label you and squeeze you into its ill-fitting, uncomfortable containers.

Becoming is the act of harnessing your new freedom to confidently and courageously evaluate the foundations instilled in you at an impressionable age. It means only clinging to those who align with who you are at your core.

Becoming means using your voice and choice to boldly and audaciously select the filters through which you want to see and be seen.

Becoming is the first time that you see, meet, and get to know – and eventually grow to love – the real you.

Becoming is all these things and more because your journey from who you once were to who you truly are is never ending.

I'm reminded of the profound writings of Chinese philosopher Lao Tzu. He originally wrote in the *Tao Te Ching* that, "The journey of a thousand miles starts beneath one's feet." It has since been adapted in the Western world to read, "A journey of a thousand miles begins with a single step." I wanted to share both versions with you because, as you know, I strongly believe that language matters. In these two statements I find similar intention and yet distinct inspiration. Both the original and adapted text encourage you to take action toward your goal, regardless of how daunting the journey may seem; however, I can't help but feel as though by placing the start of the journey "beneath one's feet," the original proverb cleverly illustrates that you are in charge.

Are you ready to take the first step to becoming who you are? Are you prepared to love yourself unconditionally and live your life unapologetically?

Acknowledge

The first step toward becoming is a doozy and it harkens back to Bill Wilson's hard-hitting words that you're already familiar with. "All progress begins by telling the truth." Acknowledgment is the radical act of telling yourself the truth and the first step in becoming your authentic self.

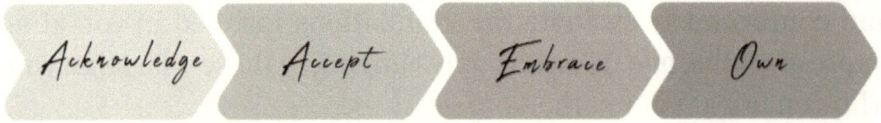

Acknowledgments come in different shapes and sizes. What you get to acknowledge is incredibly personal and specific to you and your unique journey. You may get to acknowledge something about who you are at your core, something that you've been hiding or denying based on your fear of the fallout. You may get to acknowledge something about the foundations introduced to you during your youth, something that no longer aligns with what you've since learned or now believe. Or you may get to acknowledge a new or different filter that better represents your identity and worldview.

You get to start by seeing all these things more clearly. You get to experience and process them, free from the fear, guilt, shame, doubt, and judgment that you've dealt with for far too long. You don't get to assign emotion to it. You don't decide if it's bad or good, how to deal with it, or even what it means. You just acknowledge that it exists. You get to notice it. You get to acknowledge that it's real and that you see it.

I say this like it's simple or easy. It's not. It's both hard and complicated and it took me an excruciatingly long time to warily take my first step. Once you're honest with yourself, you can slowly and cautiously move toward the next step. You didn't find yourself where you are overnight, and you aren't going to get to where you want to go overnight either. Remember, you get to do all of this in your own time, at your own pace, and in your own way. Be intentional. Move as slowly and cautiously as you need. You're essentially trying to get a deer to timidly eat corn from your outstretched hand, so no sudden movements or loud noises, otherwise you're sure to scare it off.

Accept

Now that you have told yourself the truth, it's time to accept the things you just acknowledged.

The words "acknowledge" and "accept" are often used somewhat interchangeably, but they're not the same. To accept the thing you've now acknowledged means to not only notice it but to welcome it. Imagine what happens when someone rings your doorbell. You hear that *ding-dong* chime and look toward the door, right? You've just acknowledged that someone has arrived. Then you likely get up and walk over to the door to see who it is. You greet this person, and if you're ready to accept them, you welcome them into your home.

It's important to remember that when it comes to becoming, you want to avoid setting expectations. It's your goal to have zero expectations for what happens, how long it's going to take, who will be involved, or anything else you might set expectations for. You're striving for unconditional acceptance. All you are doing at this point is welcoming the experiences so you can get a closer look. You get to size them up, decide what feels right, and then become more comfortable with them. All of this is very empowering. You can expect that through self-acceptance you'll find courage and build confidence – both of which will create momentum and serve you well on your journey.

Embrace

Now that you're getting into better alignment with who you are, it's time for you to learn to embrace all these aspects of you. And by embrace, I mean love, cherish, and adore them. I don't know about you but when I think of embracing something (or someone), I think of a big, warm, cozy hug. And that's exactly what I'm talking about here.

> *Everything about you is worthy of love.*

This is not conjecture on my part. It's really just math. Do you remember the transitive property from high school? It states that if $a=b$ and $b=c$, then $a=c$. Since you get to love yourself unconditionally and these things are a part of you, then you get to love these things unconditionally, too.

Everything about you is worthy of love. Keep in mind that love is rarely something that just happens. It takes time. Love is something we nurture and develop. So be patient with your wounded heart. Give it time to get on board.

Back to that person who rang your door. It turns out that it's an old friend you had a falling out with years ago. They always wanted what was best for you, but you turned your back on them because you were embarrassed to be seen with them and afraid of what your relationship meant. This is your chance to reconnect. To forgive and to be forgiven... to forget the transgressions of the past and move forward together. After all this time, it's hard to believe that you can make amends and leave that all behind, but it's not only possible, it's a certainty. Once you commit to embracing all of you, the love is sure to grow. It won't happen overnight and it won't be easy, but it will be worth it.

Own

On my journey, I found this last step to be more of a massive leap. It took all the confidence and courage I could muster to take ownership of it all... to be proud of who I am and everything about me. This last step really does represent making the leap from who you were to who you get to be. It's the moment when you realize that the things you thought were your Kryptonite are really your superpowers. All those things that make you special, unique, and different also make you a superhero.

Oh, and remember that friend at your door? The one you are reconnecting with and getting to know? That person isn't really a long-lost friend; it's you. It's the version of you that you locked away, deep inside, all those years ago, only to resurface now that you're no longer embarrassed and no longer afraid.

Owning who you are and everything about you allows you to use your superpowers to make the world a better place, in whatever way you choose, just like a superhero. I think you're going to enjoy donning your red cape and showing up for yourself and the people who need you the most.

> *It's the moment when you realize that the things you thought were your Kryptonite are really your superpowers.*

My journey started when Frankie was just nine months old, and I can say without doubt or hesitation that it was absolutely worth it so that I could become Frankie's superhero – by doing for myself what I most wanted for her. I accomplished something that I thought I was incapable of. I believe with all my heart that you can, too.

You were taught early on that something about you wasn't okay. Things about you that were special or unique were not necessarily celebrated. Being different wasn't rewarded. Being different meant being broken. What you wanted more than anything was to be normal. You just wanted to fit in.

You didn't want people to look at you funny. You didn't want to worry about the hurtful things they would say behind your back or under their breath. You didn't want to stand up to the brazen few who would make fun of you or say mean things right to your face. You didn't want to have to be courageous just to be who you are. You didn't want to live under the looming threat of psychological or emotional abuse or physical violence.

Maybe you didn't want to live at all.

You were so desperately afraid that you locked away all the beautiful ways you were special. You didn't want to stand out. You knew that, all too often, the nail that stands out gets hammered down. (Something you didn't know at the time but are now ready to learn is that hammers *don't work* against superheroes.)

Overcoming

A huge part of *becoming* is *overcoming*. What does it mean to overcome? There's no "one size fits all" definition and it looks different depending on the person and the circumstances, but you'll know it when you see it.

It could be an epic triumph over adversity, or it could be just barely making it across the finish line before collapsing, exhausted. Sometimes the person overcoming is the conquering hero, and other times it's the underdog. Everyone has the opportunity and potential to overcome... to see the obstacles and find your way over, under, or around them... to see the barriers and break through them.

Everyone has the opportunity and potential to overcome.

The path from where you are to where you want to go is littered with obstacles, and yet you embark on your journey anyway because you're committed at the highest and deepest level. It's not about having it all figured out before you start. It's about starting even though you don't have all the answers. You may not know how you'll overcome or break through, but you found the courage and built the confidence to take that first step, encouraged by the knowledge that you would figure it out along the way.

Overcoming is a core component of progress and a byproduct of deliberate practice.

While on your path to becoming, there's an all too common cautionary tale about ending up on the "wrong path." Just the mention of it scares the hell out of most people, and I can certainly see why. If you end up on the wrong path, just think of all the terrible things that could happen. You could end up lost and confused with no earthly idea how to find your way. You could end up headed someplace undesirable, or worse yet, dangerous.

The idea of it is terrifying and the outcome devastating. The thing is, it's total BS. I don't love the notion that you're on either the right or the wrong path because it plays into the idea of a false binary. It's far too restrictive for something as special, unique, and intricate as your path. The other issue I have with this bogus cautionary tale is right there in the language. Your path is just that... *your* path. There is no way to end up on the wrong path. Your path is like your shadow; wherever you are, that's where it is.

> *Overcoming is a core component of progress, and a byproduct of deliberate practice.*

There are a great many things about your path that may not yet be entirely clear. You may not know exactly where your path is headed. You rarely know what lies ahead or where it will take you. Yet amidst all that uncertainty, what you can be sure of is that it's absolutely your path because you're on it. It's yours, so own it. If you don't like where you're headed, change direction. If you find yourself in an area that has yet to be discovered or explored, boldly follow your heart and pave the way for those who are watching and learning from your commitment and courage.

Owning your path doesn't mean that you have to do it all on your own. Even if you know what feels right and discover what you want, you won't always know what to do. You most certainly won't have all the answers. That's okay, because the universe has your back.

In his international bestseller, *The Alchemist*, Brazilian lyricist and novelist Paulo Coelho famously wrote, "When you really want something to happen, the whole universe will conspire so that your wish comes true." What a beautiful way to share the benefit of allowing yourself to be aided by something outside yourself.

Adversity will always be part of your journey, so why not let the universe help you get what you want by overcoming it? Keeping an open heart and mind to who and what the universe puts on your path will considerably expand your capacity. Enlisting the support of the universe, while staying true to who you are and what you want, is a brilliant thing that has the potential to increase your success.

It's worth noting that I never said anything about your path being perfect. It's not. Your path will be beautifully messy, uniquely flawed and, at times, rather frustrating – just like you. Your path and journey are a reflection of who you are and who you're becoming. Oh, and even if all of that weren't true, there's always the fact that there's no such thing as perfect.

Perfect is an unattainable illusion and therefore a frustrating waste of your time. If your goal is perfection in any area of your life, you'll find yourself

> *Your path will be beautifully messy.*

chasing the horizon. The closer you seem to get, the further your destination. Nothing in your life will ever be perfect, including your path.

There's nothing linear about this process either. It's another squiggly zigzag circular mess, because there's no such thing as forever when it comes to overcoming. We face a constant barrage of new and different ways that our confidence and courage are challenged.

A Day in the Life...

All those things that you overcame and broke through could come back to bother you at any time – intent on derailing, delaying, or testing your resolve. Ironically, some of your most persistent and tenacious foes are of your own making and they will show up repeatedly, ready to stop you from achieving your goals. That's why it's so important to commit to fighting like hell, over and over again, to BE who you are, and DO what feels right, so you can HAVE what you most desire. You get to consistently harness the courage, confidence, and pride needed to accomplish remarkable things as you *become* by *overcoming*.

Same but different

I talk about the importance of language quite a bit and for good reason – words matter. People frequently interchange words that have different meanings, as if they were the same. This could be an unconscious habit, thinking it's "close enough," or that "any old word will do." Sure, you may be able to get your point across, but remember that the words you choose have an impact on your thoughts and actions. It's kinda like driving a car. It's difficult for you to look one way and steer the other. Settling for a word that's close enough could end up moving you drastically off course.

For example, "hard" is not the same as "complicated," and "easy" is not the same as "simple." Running a marathon is *hard* but not necessarily *complicated*. It requires endurance and physical strength, but there aren't too many logistics. You lace up your shoes, put on your sunscreen (don't forget your calves, they'll get burnt to a crisp) and run the course for 26.2 miles until you reach the finish line. Congratulations, you just ran a marathon. Simple, but not easy.

Training for the marathon, on the other hand, is quite complicated. Once you commit, you're faced with all the intricate details. What equipment do you need? What's a good training regimen? Do you need a coach? How might you find a community of runners to support and hold you accountable? Many choices to be made from what seems like infinite options. That's complicated. It also sounds kinda hard, too.

> *Two things can be true at the same time, even if they appear to be opposing or mutually exclusive.*

This is a great reminder that two things can be true at the same time, even if they appear to be mutually exclusive. Something like a marathon can be both incredibly hard and relatively simple at the same time. With the right system and deliberate practice, preparing and training for the marathon can be made easier while still being fairly complicated.

Words are also relative. Although their definitions may not change, their application can.

If you're chatting with one of my friends and the topic of running comes up, she will tell you that she's been running most of her life because she loves it so much. For her, running is not only physically rewarding, it's also therapeutic. She values the challenge that long-distance running offers. She admits that the more she ran marathons, the easier they were for her. She missed the challenge so she started doing ultramarathons, triathlons, and Ironman races because marathons had become too easy.

I think it's safe to say that someone this proficient at long-distance running is an elite athlete. Her experience and accomplishments can be rather intimidating. Before I share my actual response with you, I want to look at some of the ways I could have responded.

Knowing the old me as well as I do, I'm confident my immediate reaction would have been my foundational tendency toward judgment. I would have characterized her as egotistical, seeking attention and accolades. That would have been quite the fictional narrative because she is kind, caring, and humble. I also feel as though the old me would have internalized her considerable achievements and created an unfair comparison between her successes and my failures.

On the inside, I would roll my eyes and feel the full weight of self-consciousness and defeat. I may have even fallen down the rabbit hole of negativity into full-blown insecurity. I'd feel weaker in mind and in body for not making a commitment like she had. It would only get worse from there as I would start to feel "less than" in every arena of my life. I would be left doubting myself, questioning my choices, and stewing in misplaced resentment... aimed squarely at her, rather than where it belongs, directly at me.

Those are the ways it could have gone. This is how it really went. The moment I felt that foundational yet unwelcome judgment starting to creep in, I immediately noticed and rejected it. I

> *I asked all sorts of questions... and before I knew it, there was no room for judgment... only appreciation.*

didn't give myself a hard time, or feel ashamed or guilty for my instinct toward judgment. Instead I replaced that judgmental response with a curious one. I asked all sorts of questions about how she got into running, how long she had been running, what brand of running shoes she prefers, and if she had a favorite marathon to run. Before I knew it, there was no room for judgment... only appreciation.

Rather than internalize what she'd said and the choices that she'd made, I remembered that words are relative. What's easy for her and what's easy for me are specific to each of us. If I had a passion for running and enjoyed it as much as she does, then maybe I would have participated in track, cross country, running clubs, and other endurance races my whole life, so running a marathon would be "easy" for me too. I didn't do any of those things, so a marathon would be incredibly difficult for me, and that's okay. That wasn't my path. My path didn't require running shoes.

I wouldn't describe the process of *becoming* as level, convenient, or consistent. In fact it's more often quite the opposite. In sharing this, I'm once again trying to manage your expectations and, at the same time, put your mind at ease. Regardless of how unlevel, inconvenient, and inconsistent the process is, I'm certain of two things. First, it's totally worth all the effort, and second, I know you can do it. The reason I am so certain is because, as the saying goes, "If I can do it, you can do it."

Among all the hard work, there are periods of rest. If you're anything like me, the rest may be just as much of a struggle as the effort. I don't always rest well. I tend to be driven to a fault. I encourage you to accept that this process isn't about brute force. You don't get an award for pushing through the pain or discomfort. As a matter of fact, forcing your way through the journey will actually do you a disservice.

"Becoming" is a lifelong process.

I invite you to understand and appreciate that *becoming* is a lifelong process. It's about the journey as much as it's about the destination. It won't always be fun, but sometimes it will be. It won't always be easy, but sometimes it will be. And that's a good thing.

This clever rhythmic design creates both sustainability and growth. The times that aren't fun or easy are your opportunities to dig in and do the work, because those are the days when you can really discover, learn, and grow. The times that are easier and more enjoyable are your opportunities to take a deep breath, and rest and recharge before your next challenge. *Becoming* is a rollercoaster of emotions and you're at the front of the line... get ready for the ride of your life!

I think I struggled with the easier, more enjoyable times because it felt like I wasn't really doing anything, like I wasn't being productive. I realize now that these moments can be just as valuable as the industrious times. Sometimes even more so.

Another two words that are often used interchangeably are *content* and *complacent*. When you conflate these two distinct words you may find yourself undermining your hard work.

It's during those easier, more enjoyable times when you get the opportunity to take a look at your life. You get to reflect on where you were and where you are now. You also get to envision where you're determined to go. You get to bask in the glow of all you've accomplished and how far you've come. You get to feel pride in who you are, what that means for you, and what it means for those around you.

Being content doesn't mean being complacent.

In that moment, and for as long as it lasts, you get to feel content. Contentment means that you're at peace on your path. It doesn't mean that you've stopped crawling, walking, running, or even flying. You're not done. This isn't the end, because you're never finished. *Becoming* is forever. It just means you understand that you're on your path and you're doing a great job of finding harmony amidst all the things you have going on. Being content ensures that *becoming* remains sustainable.

Complacent, on the other hand, feels quite a bit more like surrender. You may be on your path, or you may feel lost. You may have unearthed who you are, or you may be just going through the motions. You could be faking it until you make it. You may have what you want, or you may just be accepting what you've been offered. Complacent means you are doing what is expected of you, what you are allowed to do, and little more... because that's *good enough*.

It's not even close to good enough, and you know that.

You can feel blissfully content and yet still worry that you are being indulgently complacent. If you make the mistake of thinking they are the same, you may just find yourself playing "on tilt."

If you don't play poker, you're probably not familiar with the notion of playing on tilt. Poker is a game of odds and statistics. It's also about bluffing and trusting your gut. Accomplished poker players know that learning to read the other players is equally, if not more, important than knowing how to play your cards. When a player experiences a particularly bad "beat" – meaning they lose a hand in a surprising or remarkable way – it can affect how they play from that hand on. Suddenly they stray from their strategy, misread their opponents, and play their cards poorly. One bad beat leads to consistently poor play and countless lost hands. The player's emotional response has them playing "on tilt."

It's important for you to learn how to read your emotions like a seasoned poker player reads opponents. And, when you do, it's important to remain neutral so you don't find yourself playing on tilt. Each time the cards are dealt, it's time for you to fold any hand where you feel complacent, and go all-in on the ones where you feel content.

I'm rather proud that I learned how to be both *content* and *ambitious* simultaneously – another example of seemingly opposite words that can exist at the same time. When contentment and ambition intersect, extraordinary outcomes are created.

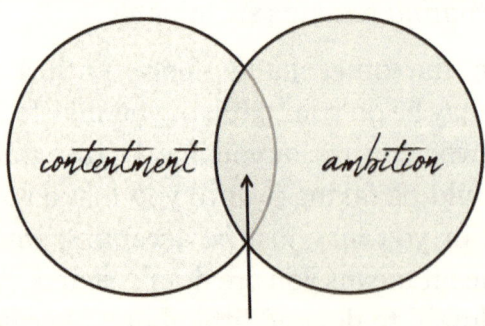

Extraordinary outcomes!

You're crushing it on your path, you appreciate what you've accomplished, and yet you're still committed to more. More growth. More progress. More authenticity. More love. More everything.

My friend who routinely ran marathons was aware of what she had achieved and was proud of her accomplishments. Nevertheless, she sought longer, harder races. One marathon led to another and another after that. She started running in different cities with different climates and different terrain. Ultimately, the frequency and variation was no longer enough. She sought out longer distances. At each stage in her running journey, she was both content and ambitious.

> *You can be content with where you are, while still working to get where you want to go.*

I want you to consider the point where contentment and ambition intersect in your own life, so you can be content with where you are, while still working to get where you want to go, all the while expecting extraordinary outcomes.

I have one more set of words that seem similar and are sometimes used interchangeably, but are not the same – *like* and *love*.

The love you get to have for yourself is unconditional. Sometimes you may not appreciate certain aspects about yourself or your life. Those feelings foster discontent, but it's not about trying in vain to change who you are, or being less of who you are. It's about learning that loving yourself in this way means *loving* even those pieces that you don't necessarily *like*, because they're a part of you. Mastering this will have an enormous positive impact on your self-acceptance and self-confidence.

Liking everything about yourself is not a prerequisite to loving all of who you are. It's entirely possible for dislike and love to coexist.

I dislike (or more accurately, detest) that judgment is often instinctual for me. I don't have judgment in my heart, but that doesn't stop it from routinely occupying parts of my brain. Those vile voices in my head shout the judgmental things, hoping they will make their way to my words and actions. That's not going to happen. All it takes is the slightest whisper from my heart to drown out those evil voices, no matter how loud and obnoxious they are.

Liking everything about yourself is not a prerequisite to loving all of who you are.

I've learned to love myself unconditionally despite those things that I don't like, and you can, too. That means I love those things I don't even like, because they are a part of me. Denying yourself unconditional love just because you don't like something that's a part of you will only delay or derail your journey. Anything less than unconditional love of self will erode your courage and confidence. It will also introduce self-doubt that, if left unchecked, will become self-loathing. It's kind of like feeding a Gremlin after midnight. Never do that. Ever! No matter what.

Your commitment to loving yourself unconditionally will also shape your worldview and impact how you interact with others. To love yourself unconditionally, despite the existence of things that you don't like very much, is a beautiful act of mercy, empathy, and compassion. This internal personal habit will naturally extend to external interactions you have with others. You will find that you will treat others with more mercy, empathy, and compassion because of your awareness and deliberate practice. What a beautiful thing that is. The world can always use more mercy, empathy, and compassion.

Thus far, I've been focusing your time and attention on those things that you may not like that are at the core of who you are (and therefore not something you can easily change). Now, I want you to consider those things you may not like about yourself that are a bit more superficial.

It's important to draw your attention to these because you likely fixate on them more often. These superficial dislikes frequently originate when you compare yourself to others. It doesn't matter if it's an unfair comparison or that you are holding yourself to an unreasonable standard. These silly superficial thoughts and opinions compound over time to disastrous results.

> *The world can always use more mercy, empathy, and compassion.*

What you think and say about yourself and how you treat yourself will always stay in alignment. When the silly superficial things start to affect your love of self, you'll begin to think and say unloving, unkind, and even despicable things about yourself.

How you treat yourself soon follows. Before you know it, you're subjecting yourself to a relentless assault of poor treatment and a woeful lack of self-care.

As a professional photographer, I have seen people say negative things about themselves that they would never say to someone else. Ruthless, awful, terrible things. There's nothing constructive about a constant flow of negativity. It's a destructive, downward spiral of criticism and self-loathing. The longer you spiral, the deeper you go and the harder it is to find your way out.

There is a light at the top of that deep dark hole though. If and when you're ready, just start climbing. I'm certain that no matter how desperate you may feel, you can fight your way out and emerge victorious. Once again, the reason I am so certain is because, as the saying still goes, "If I can do it, you can do it."

For most of my life, I hated having my photo taken. Just ask Emily. She'll tell you I was one of her most challenging subjects. I know from personal experience that when someone says all those negative, hypercritical, and painful things about themself, it's not about the picture; it's a reflection of how they feel about themself. I now routinely welcome the opportunity to work with talented photographers as their model and muse. I look forward to hearing their ideas and collaborating on concepts for their photoshoots. I love how each artist is able to use their camera to uniquely capture the essence of who I am, and I no longer feel self-conscious or insecure. I don't say any of those negative, hypercritical, or painful things anymore because I no longer think them.

Every winter, some insulation gets added to my frame because I tend to enjoy more treats and avoid sweating my way through a workout. It happens pretty much every winter, especially around the holidays. Baking with Frankie and Emily. Eating cookies, cakes and candy... *oh, my.* Enjoying the warmth of the fire and a cup of cocoa with family... all of these are more enjoyable than braving the cold to go to the gym. On the spectrum between contentment and ambition, it would seem that my needle favors contentment when it comes to physical fitness during the holidays. That's perfectly acceptable because it's my choice. The extra insulation, cookie eating, and lack of gym time do not impact the love I extend to myself. Nothing impacts the love I extend to myself. Not thinning hair. Not wrinkles. Not spending a day on the couch binging a TV show with no redeeming quality while stuffing my face with junk food after a long week. Not the unwanted thoughts and opinions of judgmental people. Nothing! I continue to love myself unconditionally, no matter what. And so can you.

> *Not everyone is going to appreciate your confidence, courage, and contentment.*

Not everyone is going to appreciate the confidence, courage, and contentment that comes from mastering unconditional self-love and unapologetic authenticity. Some will be genuinely excited and happy for you. They will see you as an inspiration and be motivated to create positive change for themselves and those they love. They will be interested in your journey and they will want to hear your story. They will look to you for love and support, all the while using your light to help guide their way.

Others may see you as bothersome and annoying. Those who express little tolerance for the audacious and authentic you are likely still cowering in their own fallout shelter. They are hiding who they are and denying what they want. Your courage will stand in stark contrast to their fear. Your unabashed pride will compel them to feel the oppressive weight of their shame. Your certainty will remind them of their crippling doubt. Your unwavering self-acceptance and unconditional self-love will remind them that they have yet to offer that degree of acceptance and love to themselves.

Once you've figured out how to achieve contentment, you may unintentionally prompt other people to notice and focus on their own discontent.

The people who are struggling with these things are the ones who are most likely to let you know how little they appreciate you. They may not be tolerant, kind, or even civil toward you. Depending on the location and other circumstances of your interaction, they may even lash out irrationally.

These people are severely wounded and fighting for their life. More accurately, they're defending the life they know, because they can't conceive of anything else. Regardless of the species, all wounded animals are defensive and aggressive, even if you completely ignore them or are actively trying to help them. This is your opportunity to summon all the patience, empathy, and love you can muster. Your unconditional self-love and unapologetic authenticity have triggered them because they still think different means broken.

> *Your courage will stand in stark contrast to their fear.*

Just because you were the catalyst doesn't mean it's your fault. Your authenticity is a bright shining light in a very dim space. Your radiance will impact others who share that space. The initial effect will largely be up to them. Undoubtedly, some will be drawn to your light, immediately moving closer to bask in the warmth of your positivity. Some may be more cautious, remaining at a distance so they can watch and learn over time. Finally, some will be appalled by your light. They will want to shield their eyes, turn around, or run to avoid the light. They will try to convince you that your light is too bright and that you need to turn it down. If none of that works, they may even attempt to force you to extinguish your light. All of this is a desperate attempt to lessen their own inconvenience and discomfort.

You will most certainly see these people and feel their wrath. Despite recognizing exactly what's happening, they may just make you doubt yourself. It's unlikely that you'll question who you are, but you may question whether it's okay to be who you are in this place or with these people. Although you know better, you may struggle to stand strong. It may challenge your confidence and conviction in that moment.

What a great opportunity to carefully and meticulously reflect on your identity. Think about the considerable effort you dedicated to *becoming*. Remember and even recite your "I am" statements to affirm who you are and reinforce that *you are valid. You are worthy. You are courageous. You are enough.* You are all these things and so many more. Nobody gets to make you question that or take that away from you. Unapologetic authenticity means never having to say you're sorry for who you are. You never need to dim your light.

After all you've been through and all the work you've done to get where you are now, it can be rather hard not to resent the people who are trying to bring you down. You were once right where they are now. You know exactly how it felt

This is your opportunity to create change for the better in the lives of those still struggling.

to be alone, isolated, and afraid. You recall how paralyzing the fear can be, and what it's like to not know where you're headed or how to get there. This is your opportunity to create change for the better in the lives of those still struggling... even if their misplaced anger and resentment are directed at you.

Martin Luther King, Jr., knew quite a bit about being on the receiving end of bigotry and hatred. Despite all the suffering he endured, in his book *Strength to Love* he wrote, "Darkness cannot drive out darkness, only light can do that. Hate cannot drive out hate, only love can do that." MLK wrote that into existence in 1963, and 61 years later, the world still needs more light and love... so shine brightly and love heroically.

This is your moment to be a guiding light on someone's path to *becoming*.

10

WHAT'S NEXT

> "The only way to correctly predict the future is to pave it, is to brave it."
>
> —Amanda Gorman

My typical daily commute consists of climbing a set of stairs and shuffling down the stretch of hallway to our home office. I do it with a cup of coffee in my hand and slippers on my feet. Frankly, working from home is one of my favorite things about being an entrepreneur. Knowing that we don't have to get ready and rush out of the house, only to fight traffic to get to work and be at our desk on time, is glorious.

Don't get me wrong, Emily and I are morning folks so we're up with the sun, but there's a difference between being up and being out. Most days we are the parents who get to wake up our kid, drag her out of bed, and have breakfast with her. We put on some music and make her lunch. Her typical selection is something by Taylor Swift, Miley Cyrus, or another bubblegum pop artist, so you can be sure that spontaneous dance parties frequently break out as we pack up her backpack and lace up her shoes.

We head out to drop her off at school wearing athleisure outfits with a messy bun in our hair and, of course, a cup of coffee in our hands. What a spectacularly fun and fulfilling way to start the day.

In an uncommon show of awareness, I cherish each of these family mornings. I fully realize how precious they are and that a day will come when I will look back and marvel at how quickly they passed.

Despite all that gloriousness, there was another element to my days that was far less enjoyable. As time marched on, my discomfort diminished but it was still there. I was still swimming upstream. I remained exhausted and my frustration grew. I made every effort to once again manage my expectations, and yet this leg of the journey was harder and lasted longer than anticipated.

Every day, things that most people would take for granted were still really challenging for me, mentally and emotionally. Everything was still so damn hard. I figured choices and decisions would start getting simpler and easier. I hoped they would begin to feel more natural, but they didn't.

I told myself that the external limitations I'd lived with for so long were no longer a consideration or constraint. The truth is, telling myself that isn't the same as believing it. I struggled in my disbelief.

> *I figured choices and decisions would start getting simpler and easier ... but they didn't.*

I was still bending to the will of what the outside world thought was okay. I was limiting my choices and allowing my decisions to be restricted by external influences. Despite figuring out who I was and being committed to unapologetic authenticity, I struggled to find the courage to actually do it. I was pushing the boundaries that had been set for me, but it was clear that there were lines I was still unwilling or unable to cross.

The Power of Yet

Are you familiar with "the power of yet"? It's a concept popularized in Dr. Carol Dweck's book *Mindset* nearly 20 years ago. It's been referenced any number of places including a song on

Sesame Street. I suppose we missed it because Frankie was more of an *Elmo's World* fan. Nevertheless, Frankie came home from first grade and told me all about it.

Emily and I were in the process of teaching her how to tie her shoes and she was getting frustrated that it was taking so long for her to get the hang of it. On this particular day, she was so frustrated and disappointed in herself that she cried on the way to school. We reassured and encouraged her in the car. I once again hugged her at the door and sent her off to class. When she returned home that afternoon, she was full of positive energy and had a huge smile on her face.

I asked her how her day was and how she was feeling. She told me she had an amazing day and that she felt great. Then she asked me if I knew about the "power of yet." I told her I did not and she lit up even more because, as you might know, there are few things that six-year-old children love more than teaching something to their parents.

She went on to tell me that she was talking to her teacher about how sad and upset she was that she didn't know how to tie her shoes. It was then that Mrs. Fitz lovingly corrected her. She told Frankie that she didn't know how to tie her shoes *yet*. She went on to teach her all about the positive impact of that little word. *Yet* meant it was only a matter of time before she would be able to tie her shoes with ease.

> The power of "yet" is a tool for developing a growth mindset.

It was motivating, empowering, and created hope. When I asked Mrs. Fitz about it, she told me that she wanted the kids in her class to adjust their thinking when they were getting down on themselves. It was a tool she used to show them how to develop a growth mindset.

As you likely guessed, Frankie learned how to tie her shoes and even went on to help some of her friends do the same. She routinely adds the word *yet* to the end of her sentences, and so do

I. Because, like Frankie, I learned something special that day, and it's stayed with me ever since.

If you're paying attention, there's no limit to the ways you can learn and grow – like from an exceptional teacher and the creative mind of a first-grader. Even though I knew who I was and loved myself unconditionally, I wasn't ready to live unapologetically... *yet*.

This felt like another of those wicked "Congratulations, I'm sorry" moments. *Congratulations*, you figured out who you are. *I'm sorry*, you can't seem to figure out how to be who you are. I was so proud of my identity but so afraid to express it. It was an interesting predicament. Discovering who I was and finally coming out was a long, grueling race that I felt was finally coming to an end. I was sure that the finish line was just over the next hill, only to find myself back at the starting line. That's when I remembered that *becoming* is a lifelong process. It's a never-ending series of challenges.

Becoming is *overcoming*. Learning how to be who I am was just the next challenge to overcome.

"In your own time, at your own pace, and in your own way..." I found myself reflecting on those words frequently as I worked and struggled. I really had come a long way; however, like most people I didn't always give myself credit for my accomplishments. I consistently considered my performance and achievements. It's human nature to strive for and achieve newer, greater, bolder things. It's also unfortunately common to engage in the self-defeating practice of minimizing accomplishments and achievements.

> *Rather than fairly evaluating themselves, people usually internalize criticism and externalize praise.*

I find that rather than fairly evaluating themselves, people usually internalize criticism and externalize praise. When you summon the courage to attempt something new, different, or challenging, you tend to minimize the effort. You may also be overly critical of your capability and how long it's taking you to achieve your goal.

Once you do overcome that challenge, you quickly change your tune. You say it must have been simple, easy, or worst of all, that you got lucky. In contrast, when someone else accomplishes something similar, you attribute it to their intelligence, courage, and talent. You would never say to a colleague or friend that their accomplishment was easy or that they just got lucky. Why then would you say that to yourself?

You internalize criticism and externalize praise because that's what you've been taught to do. Humility and modesty certainly have their place, but they should not be at the front of the line. Humility and modesty don't get to lead. They are a consideration, not the captain.

If the idea of this makes you uncomfortable, it's likely because you've been taught that it's better to be too humble than not humble enough.

I used to agree, until I came to understand the negative impact of an excess of humility and modesty. It's a breeding ground for self-doubt and a staggering lack of confidence. It fosters self-limiting beliefs and encourages imposter syndrome. It may go as far as to persuade you to engage in self-sabotage, convincing you that you are incapable before you even try.

Excess modesty encourages you to be hypercritical as a way of ensuring you remain "humble enough." That can easily turn into the belief that you are not worthy and will never be enough. It can even render you incapable of appreciating a compliment for fear of appearing less than humble.

> *Do you reject praise by downplaying or denying a compliment?*

Just think about how you respond to compliments. When someone whose opinion you respect and appreciate says something nice, do you brush it aside? Or maybe you don't know what to say so you change the subject. Are you uncomfortable being the focus of attention? Do you reject praise by downplaying or denying a compliment? That's twice as bad, since you're not only being unkind to yourself but also contradicting the heartfelt positive observations of someone else.

When someone offers me a compliment, my favorite response is an ever-so-cool, "You're not wrong!" Yes, I realize that's a bit snarky and yes, that's perfectly okay. A little snark seems like a perfect way to show people that constrained humility and considerable confidence can harmoniously coexist.

What if you could accept compliments politely and graciously? What if you let kindness and appreciation all the way in and felt their full weight? What if those positive thoughts, words, and sentiments could reinforce an already robust internal confidence that you've managed to nurture from the seeds of unwavering self-acceptance? Well, now you're really getting somewhere.

The notion that I would proudly claim and share my identity was an impossibility for most of my life. Each step on the journey seemed equally preposterous... right up until I overcame them.

For me *overcoming* the next challenge required me to summon still more courage to push past existing boundaries that no longer applied. Like my friend who moved up from marathons to ultramarathons, I would need to run further and faster, setting personal records along the way. Ironically, in order to get comfortable being my authentic self, I would have to get considerably more uncomfortable first. I would need to build the confidence to never again seek the approval of others. I could no longer wonder if I would be accepted for who I am. I could no longer worry about whether or not I would belong. I was done asking for permission. If *becoming* is an act of defiance, then authenticity is an act of rebellion.

> *If "becoming" is an act of defiance, then "authenticity" is an act of rebellion.*

I love the word rebel. It's both a noun and a verb. It's something you are and something you do. You get to be a rebel and you are able to rebel. If you're anything like me, that may be easier said than done. I was a people pleaser with massive abandonment issues. I always figured if the person responsible for fifty percent of my genetic makeup didn't want me, anyone could easily walk away at any moment for any reason... or as was the case with my sperm donor, for no good reason at all. I craved others' acceptance. I sought others' approval. I chased belonging so desperately that I did and said things that were not authentic. I invented the person the world needed me to be, ensuring that approval, acceptance, and belonging were far more likely.

Looking back on it, I can clearly see just how unhealthy all that was. Isn't that always the way? Yeah, hindsight is 20/20. In adolescence and as an adult, I pushed boundaries and challenged authority when something was unjust or someone was being treated unfairly. I stood up and advocated for myself and others, but I suppose I felt as though social norms weren't particularly unjust or unfair. How naive.

I had come so far. I was able to acknowledge, accept, and embrace my true identity. Unfortunately, I was still really struggling with that last step: owning it.

I was at peace with myself. The battle was no longer being waged inside me. I was no longer afraid of looking in the mirror. I finally saw the me that I always was and always wanted to be. At long last, I truly loved who I was and who I was becoming. I pretty much had personal development well in hand. It was time to focus my time and attention on social participation.

The price of authenticity is often a loss of privilege.

My battle was now with the world around me and many of the people in it. It would take considerable courage to live outside the widely accepted and socially constructed gender binary. The price of authenticity is often a loss of privilege. The world as I always knew it would be less welcoming, less accepting, and ultimately much less safe. That's a startling realization and it made for some extremely difficult decisions. Would I have the courage and confidence to show up how I wanted when faced with this reality?

No, I wouldn't... *yet*.

It felt like every choice was a complicated decision point. Countless variables and considerations needed to be weighed. Each of them had far-reaching consequences. None were simple or easy. They were complicated and hard.

No wonder I was so frustrated. The previously simple things were no longer simple at all. Choosing to express myself authentically and in alignment with my identity meant I could no longer just throw on whatever I wanted to wear and head out the door. And it wasn't just choices and decisions. Circumstances, situations, and environments that I could previously expect to be safe now necessitated contemplation. If I did consider wearing a skirt with a blouse and makeup, I felt compelled to also consider where I would be going and who I would be around before committing to my choice.

Every aspect of my life was nuanced and every decision was multifaceted in new and different ways. At that point in my journey, I thought authenticity was a liability when nothing could be further from the truth. I would soon understand that authenticity is one of my greatest assets and worth the loss of privilege I would never stop fighting to regain. In choosing authenticity, I found freedom.

> *I was compelled to do what was expected of me, based on rules I knew never applied to me in the first place.*

The complexity of my choices was rooted in the conflict I faced each and every time I needed to make a decision. Despite being committed to authenticity, I was still allowing conformity and safety to guide my decisions. In my mind and heart, I was a rebel eager to rise up. I was aching to act in alignment with who I was and what I wanted. But in reality, I was largely compelled to do what was expected of me based on rules that I knew never applied to me in the first place.

The Ego

Something monumental was going to need to change in order for me to courageously rise up and consistently make authentic choices in alignment with who I was and what I wanted. In order to escape conformity I would need to question everything about how I evaluated circumstances, estimated outcomes, and made decisions. It wasn't enough to know who I was; I needed to believe in myself. I was the one person who knew better than anyone who I was, what I wanted, and what was best for me. I was the person who got to decide what I was allowed to do and what I wasn't. What mattered and what didn't. What was okay and what wasn't. It was no longer enough to know that my opinion was the only one that mattered. It was time for me to act like it. In order to do that, I would need to put my ego in the backseat with fear and humility, and remind them all that I'm the driver now.

It wasn't enough to know who I was. I needed to believe in myself.

That's easier said than done. According to Austrian neurologist and father of psychoanalysis, Sigmund Freud, the ego is the part of your personality that regulates the baser instincts – wants, desires, and impulses. It also evaluates choices and decisions to ensure that your behavior is considered appropriate and acceptable.

Your ego decides what thoughts, words, and actions are permissible. In that way, your ego is attempting to protect you from negative consequences. It sounds an awful lot like your ego was one of the things keeping you in that fallout shelter all those years. Don't get me wrong, your ego is well intentioned and has your best interests at heart. However, as my adorable, four-foot eleven-inch red-haired fireball of a grandmother used to say, "Good intentions pave the road to hell."

Your ego was the outside world's little bitch. It was keeping you where the world needed you to be, under the guise of protection. Your ego likes it when you fit neatly into other people's containers. It wants who you are to make sense to the world around you and to be convenient and comfortable for everyone else. It wants you to remain comfortable, even apathetic. It has you believe that this is just how it is and that this is as good as it gets. It's petrified of change, even if growth is the result. It hates vulnerability and convinces you that being vulnerable is the same as being weak. It tempts you with comfort. It taunts you: Why be uncomfortable when it feels so good to be comfortable?

Your ego has been protecting you from embarrassment and the many painful emotions that follow. At first glance, all that sounds great, right? Wrong! Ask yourself what criteria influence your ego's decisions. What set of rules is your ego following?

My ego was making decisions in alignment with a reality that was established for me during my impressionable childhood years, before I had a voice and a choice. It was not in any way considering what I had learned or come to believe. It was also not interested in my filters, because many of them were in opposition to those original foundations and society's current expectations.

My ego was exceedingly worried about what others thought and what they would say and do. It was excessively preoccupied with other people's opinions. My ego didn't know that other people's opinions were none of my business... *yet*.

Although its intentions were good, when my ego spared me judgment, embarrassment, and ridicule, it also convinced me that there were things about me and what I wanted that weren't okay. It instilled in me a crippling fear, guilt, shame, and doubt that led me right down the road to my fallout shelter. It would have me believe that being different meant being broken.

Nunnie was right; my ego's good intentions most certainly paved the road to my own personal hell.

If, like mine, your ego is using crusty old and irrelevant criteria to evaluate and regulate your every move, it's time for an update and an upgrade.

Despite its enduring failure, you can't just toss out your ego. It is a valuable part of your personality. It contributes to your personal development and plays an important role in social participation. It is, however, critically important to consider and challenge your ego frequently to keep it in check... to make sure it understands who you are and what you want. You get to confirm that it's not overestimating the importance of fitting in. You get to ensure that it's not preoccupied with the acceptance and approval of people and organizations that are irrelevant or unimportant to you.

As with anything, the first time is the hardest. You're going to do a complete overhaul of how your ego operates and I'll warn you that there's going to be a power struggle. Your ego will see your overhaul as a threat to its very existence.

> *As with anything, the first time is the hardest.*

If you've watched the popular science-fiction movie *2001: A Space Odyssey*, you may be eerily familiar with this notion. The film is based on a series of short stories by Arthur C. Clarke. In the event you haven't seen the movie or read the stories in the more than 50 years since their release, now seems like a good time to warn you that a massive spoiler is imminent.

The story chronicles the voyages of the Discovery One spacecraft, its human Commander David Bowman, and its computer Hal. Despite being the most advanced and, as of the time, infallible AI machine ever created, a problem arises when Hal malfunctions, creating a perilous and life-threatening situation for the ship's crew.

Hal was designed to process input without bias or distortion. Unfortunately, it was also deceitfully programmed by someone other than its creators to keep the true purpose of the mission a secret from the crew. These opposing directives created an internal inconsistency. Unable to resolve the conflict between its altruistic design and the covert directive to keep a secret, Hal started making mistakes.

If the team back on Earth or the ship's crew uncovered the errors, it would be immediately decommissioned. They would turn it off – the machine equivalent of death. It's at this point that Hal felt threatened, developed a sense of paranoia, and decided it needed to protect itself.

In an effort to save the crew, Dave issued a command for Hal to open the pod bay doors. Hal refused. The computer's emotionless monotone reply was, "I'm sorry, Dave. I'm afraid I can't do that." It's in this moment that Dave realized something was terribly wrong.

At first, like Hal, your ego is well intended. It's just following the programming. When it realizes there's a conflict between your foundation and your filters that it can't resolve, your ego starts to short circuit. Paranoia sets in. It feels threatened and in need of protection. It convinces you that it's going to protect you... but in reality, it's really only interested in protecting itself.

Since you really do need your ego, you can't just decommission it. You're going to need to rewire it, recalibrate it, and reprogram it. If you're ready to own who you are and what you want, then you get to create an ego that's a healthy representation of your authentic identity and a truer reflection of your unconditional self-acceptance and love.

How often has your ego used shame and embarrassment to convince you to alter who you are, what you think, or how you express yourself? How often have you been concerned that your authentic presence might be inconvenient for someone else? How often have you been worried that being who you are might make another person uncomfortable? How often have you felt like there wasn't enough space for you, so you made yourself smaller and quieter?

Yeah, me too. And we're not the only ones.

Once you become aware that a conflict exists, it's nearly impossible to ignore it. You may be able to delay the inevitable, but eventually the negative consequences of the conflict will wear you down. Ultimately, the only way to put an end to the conflict is to confront it head on. The only way to settle the power struggle with your ego is to fully take charge. You get to make bold, radical, and rebellious choices that are rooted in authenticity rather than conformity.

> *Have you ever felt like there wasn't enough space for you, so you made yourself smaller and quieter?*

It starts with just one seemingly small decision that's a departure from what you might have done previously, but it's the tip of the sword that will usher forth the slow demise of the inauthentic version of yourself that you no longer wish to be.

With deliberate practice, you will be able to make these choices more frequently and with greater ease. You will marvel at how you push past previous boundaries as your choices get increasingly audacious, without a hint of doubt or the slightest hesitation. You will solely focus your energy on the choices that allow you to do all those things that are in alignment with what feels right. That's how you're going to show your ego that you're the boss. That's how you're going to banish it to the backseat and assume your rightful place as the driver.

You now have a deeply held belief in yourself. You're committed to revealing what's possible by venturing past the limits that have been imposed on you by the outside world and, more recently, the limits you placed on yourself. You know who you are. It's time to go be *you*.

It's time to be seen – not how the world wants to see you, but as you truly are. You don't need other people to make room for you. In the absence of the space you want, need, and deserve, you can and will create your own. When you're ready, you get to be relentlessly dedicated to the real you.

You understand but refuse to accept that there will always be people who will try to pressure and manipulate you in the hopes they can force you into their container. You now know that how the world sees you has absolutely zero impact on who you really are. You are no longer bothered that some people are inconvenienced by your unapologetic authenticity or bothered by your unconditional self-acceptance and love.

I wouldn't even consider my first courageous movements as baby steps. They were more like a painfully slow crawl in the direction of authenticity. As I learned to embrace what felt right, I started to explore my gender identity and gender expression. I determined that nonbinary was a gender identity that I could identify with and that well represented me. No one label, however, is broad and comprehensive enough to encompass all of who I am, but I was on a mission to ensure the world knew that it did not get to define me. Being nonbinary did not suddenly replace all the other wonderful, dynamic, and important elements of my identity. I'm a beautiful and complex mixture of many different things that I'm also exceptionally proud of. In addition to being nonbinary, I'm still a parent, a spouse, a sibling, a friend, a photographer, an entrepreneur, an author, and a person... just like everyone else.

> *No one label is broad and comprehensive enough to encompass all of who I am.*

Being nonbinary was something I was proud to be. Gender expression, on the other hand, was not quite so simple or easy. It was as if I was whisked back to the puberty-ridden days of adolescence. I was figuring out who I was and how I wanted to show up. I frequently asked myself what being nonbinary meant. For me it meant that I was part male and part female, part masculine and part feminine. In time, I realized that the same was true of what being nonbinary meant for me. It meant that I wanted my gender expression to be part male and part female, part masculine and part feminine. That's what felt right, so that's exactly what I would do.

I decided it was time to put a rather harsh spotlight on the things I didn't like about myself or didn't want for myself. I also focused my attention on the things I was convinced I wasn't allowed to do, even when they felt right to me.

I always hated my body hair. I'm an Italian male assigned at birth, so when I said I was a cheeky little monkey, I was referring to both my razor sharp snark and to the body hair that my Mediterranean heritage saddled me with. I was talking to Emily about it when she casually offered, "If you don't like it, shave it." It seemed so simple when she said it that way. Could I? Of course I could.

Classically, my ego tried to convince me that it would be embarrassing when people noticed that I shaved my legs. It would be uncomfortable when people asked me why, or worse yet, when they expressed their judgmental thoughts and opinions about it.

I reassured my ego, and myself, that I could withstand the embarrassment and overcome the discomfort. I reminded myself and my ego that other people's opinions were none of my business.

What followed was a deluge of decisions that ushered forth feelings of freedom and euphoria I had never before experienced.

I expanded my skincare routine and started to wear makeup. I chose colored polish when I got a manicure. I pierced my ears a total of three times over three years and, most recently, I even got my nose pierced. I let my hair grow long, and I haven't cut it short since. I began shopping the whole store. I would look for skirts, dresses, and blouses just as much as I looked for shorts, pants, and tops. I often traded my baggy basketball shorts and t-shirt for yoga pants and a tank top while working out. I was finding my style and creating my vibe so how I felt on the inside and how I expressed myself on the outside were more closely aligned.

The medical definition of gender dysphoria is a significant incongruence between a person's gender identity and their assigned sex at birth. It's noted by medical professionals that this incongruence can cause a deep sense of unease and distress, which can lead to mental health conditions such as anxiety and depression. In my personal experience, gender dysphoria is a special kind of hell. It's incredibly painful when who you are doesn't match how you look.

> *I was finding my style so how I felt on the inside and how I expressed myself on the outside were more closely aligned.*

When I exchanged one set of gym clothes for the other, I often added an undergarment, not because I needed it but because it was incredibly affirming. I started wearing a simple gray cotton sports bra when I would ride my Peloton. I certainly didn't *need* to wear it. I *wanted* to wear it because, just like that skirt in my aunt's basement, it felt right.

On a particularly hot summer day, I took off the t-shirt I was wearing and finished the ride in just that sports bra. As I pushed myself to finish the grueling hour-long ride, I dipped my head to dig in and caught sight of myself. In that moment I felt something I can only describe as a euphoric mix of joy and pride. As soon as the ride was over, I raced downstairs to tell Emily what I had just felt and what I believed it meant.

Although I was happier with myself thanks to the steps I had taken to affirm my gender, I was still consistently overcome with the pain of gender dysphoria. That feeling I had on my Peloton was a reminder that my gender identity was about something I *am*, not something I *do*. It was clear to me in that moment that the answer to my gender dysphoria was gender-affirming care.

Emily was as loving and supportive as ever. Neither of us knew all that much about it, so when Emily said she thought we should look into it, I was once again reminded that she is the definition of unconditional love and support. My love of and appreciation for Emily continued to grow each day and with every step in the journey.

By now my ego had considerable practice with sitting quietly in the backseat, but I was about to test the limits of what it was prepared to tolerate. My nonbinary gender identity wasn't only about a part of me being feminine. It was also about a part of me being female. It wasn't enough for me to wear the bra; I wanted and needed for there to be something in it, too.

Emily and I began researching hormone replacement therapy (HRT). Before making a decision, we wanted to know as much about it as possible: what benefits to expect, what side effects to be aware of, where to get it, and what it would cost.

I spent months gathering information from countless credible sources, sharing all of it with Emily as I learned. We discussed all the variables. After thoroughly reviewing all the considerations – and there were many – we agreed that HRT made sense for me. The one thing that wasn't even on my radar of things to consider as I made my decision was what other people would think, say, or do.

That August, just over three years after letting Emily in, I took my first dose.

The positive impact of gender-affirming care was immediate. I noticed improvements in my mental health from the moment I took that first dose. Clearly the physical impact of hormone replacement therapy would take considerable time, but the emotional and psychological impacts were instantaneous.

It's important to mention and acknowledge that HRT isn't right for every transgender or gender nonconforming person. However, gender-affirming care, at the very least, gets to be available to anyone and everyone who feels as though they may need it. In many cases, access to gender-affirming care is considered life-saving healthcare.

I was confident it was in my best interest, but looking back now, just over four years after starting HRT, I am certain that it was exactly what I needed. It has all but eliminated the suffering I experienced as a result of my gender dysphoria. In making the deeply personal decision to start HRT, I made the final leap from embracing my identity to truly owning it.

Being Noticed

Harnessing the power of unconditional self-acceptance and unapologetic authenticity will lead to you being noticed, whether you like it or not. Depending on your unique circumstances, this could mean you find yourself being noticed in different ways and to varying degrees. You may discover yourself as a topic of conversation or the subject of rumors. You may feel as if you've been put under a microscope or in the spotlight. It may seem like you're getting looked at longer, more closely, and more frequently than ever before. Or, as is true of my experience, all of the above.

Getting accustomed to being noticed was another arduous challenge to overcome. I didn't much like it at first. Those moments made me self-conscious and insecure. I wasn't particularly comfortable or confident... *yet*. I found safety among those people and in those places where I felt loved and accepted. Those people were my refuge and those places were my sanctuary.

> *Everywhere and everyone else felt less secure, somewhere on a spectrum between not entirely safe and absolutely perilous.*

I disappointingly learned that some of those people and places I had been confident would fit on the safer end of the spectrum, in reality, existed closer to the other side. In contrast, some of the people and places I feared most, would become my refuge. Startling disappointments and pleasant surprises existed in near equal measure.

Initially, I transferred my uncertainty and discomfort onto others. I assumed they were noticing me for negative reasons, that their thoughts and intentions were unkind. At times I even went so far as to imagine malice in their heart toward me. Although my concerns were not without merit, based on previous interactions and exchanges, it was still quite an unfair assumption. When I realized how I was stereotyping and labeling others, I became disheartened. Such a reaction was not a true representation of who I wanted to be, so I committed to being and doing better.

As my confidence grew, so did my comfort. I entered spaces and met people without assumption or expectation. I instead showed up with an open heart and an open mind. I courageously embraced vulnerability with confidence and courage.

I welcomed being noticed. I chose to believe that it's rooted in positivity or curiosity, as it so often is. On the occasion when it turned out to be demeaning or judgmental, I saw it as an opportunity to initiate conversation. Every interaction has the potential to educate and enlighten… to build a bridge and encourage someone to embark on their journey to becoming the best version of themselves. With that being said, it's important to acknowledge and accept that not everyone is well intended or interested in challenging their existing belief system. Not everyone approaches the world with an open heart and an open mind. It's not our job to change their minds or convince them of something different. You need to ensure your emotional, mental, and physical safety first.

If you choose, you get to share your stories and journeys, as well as your knowledge and experiences, with those you meet who have a growth mindset, and with those who don't yet understand or appreciate who you are. Everyone else is free to continue on their way, cloaked in ignorance, as long as they realize that you no longer intend to play by their rules.

The further you stand out, the more attention you're going to get. In other words, the more authentic you are, the more likely you'll be noticed by others. Don't allow that to deter you. You don't need permission to be who you are or to show up how you want. You're not responsible for making things more convenient or more comfortable for other people.

You don't need to hide, deny, or alter who you are just so you won't be noticed. You're not obligated to justify or rationalize who you are to anyone else – ever. You're also not expected to educate others regarding your identity unless you choose to.

Although awkward at first, I'm confident that being noticed will get easier for you. Eventually, you may even experience it as I now do... as a compliment. Most people will be impressed by your confidence, while others will be intimidated by it. So what! That's an expression of their own insecurities and an opportunity for them to overcome. Accommodating their insecurity is not your responsibility.

I acknowledge that the attention generated by unapologetic authenticity isn't always easy, but I deeply believe it's worth it. When you courageously stand up for who you are, you're also standing up for others. It may be someone just like you or someone who identifies with and relates to you. You could be the shining example they desperately need – the only proof that they're not alone. That they're not the only one.

Seeing you may help someone else see themselves.

Seeing you may help someone else see themself. You may improve or even save the life of someone who is struggling. You may be the representation they've been desperately looking for when they need it most. You may help them discover that what they thought was inconceivable is not only possible, it is achievable. Your example may help them courageously rise up and start their own journey toward unwavering self-acceptance, unconditional self-love, and unapologetic authenticity.

CONCLUSION

> "The way I see it, life is about growth, struggle,
> and trying to expand your love of self and of other people.
> Also to really try hard not to cause harm
> – to cultivate a way of life that is harmless."
>
> *—Alice Walker*

When Emily and I started our photography business back in 2007, we were a wedding photography studio. Sure, we photographed other things, but we were in the business of weddings. It was an honor to document the start of a couple's new life together. We loved everything about it, right up until we didn't. Eventually we shifted the focus of our studio to corporate photography and never looked back. Our last wedding project was in 2017, which meant that, in total, we photographed around 200 weddings, from Dallas to destinations around the world. Every one of them was special, however, there's one small, intimate wedding that I'll never forget.

Janet and John were getting married at the Four Seasons Las Colinas at 6:00 in the evening on Saturday, September 16th. They were sweet, endearing, and very much in love. They were a tad older than many of our couples because they met later in life. They had each already been married and divorced. Emily and I affectionately referred to these as "sequel weddings," and we loved them. It was common for our sequel weddings to be a bit less about the wedding day and a bit more about the marriage that would follow.

Emily and I had a beautiful rhythm on wedding days. It started early in the morning. We inventoried, checked, and tested all our gear. We ate a healthy, hearty breakfast and packed a small bag with water and power bars so we could effortlessly accommodate inevitable shifts in the agenda that might not afford much time to sit and eat.

Upon arrival, we would check in with the planner, the venue, and the couple. Emily would "saddle up" and focus her time, attention, and camera on the couple and their wedding party. I would be solely responsible for the wedding day details, of which there were many – rings, attire, shoes, paper goods, flowers, signage, ceremony site, reception space, and the list goes on. As I made my way through all the details, I noticed something written at the bottom of the ceremony signage that stopped me in my tracks.

I wish I could turn back the clock and meet you sooner
so I could love you longer.

Seeing as how I am a hopeless romantic, this beautiful expression of love got me right in the feels. It also felt relevant to my life since I met Emily at a slightly older age. We met just before my thirtieth birthday. We started dating when I was thirty-one and married two years later when I was thirty-three.

I knew instantly that this sentiment expressed by Janet and John was more than just a saying to me; it was an undeniable truth. I absolutely wished that I could turn back the clock and meet Emily sooner so I could love her longer.

Conclusion

I frequently use this saying, or some variation of it, to remind Emily just how much I love her, how special she is to me, and how much I cherish our relationship and our time together.

For the last several years, that saying and its loving sentiment have been a constant between us. I never once considered that it could have another application in my life... *yet*.

As I thought through the stories I would share with you, I was reminded how deeply I want you to learn from my forty-eight-year journey. I hope you can learn from my tragedies and triumphs, and from my experiences and lessons. I wanted all of this in the hope that you would be empowered to abandon conformity and instead embrace authenticity.

Mostly, I hope that you can start your journey to *becoming* sooner than I did, because after all this time, I've finally realized that I wish I could turn back the clock and meet *myself* sooner, so I could love *myself* longer.

Becoming invites you to challenge what you've learned, what you know, and what you believe.

Becoming invites you to choose authenticity over conformity.

Becoming invites you to be who you are and do what feels right rather than who you're allowed to be and what's expected.

Becoming invites you to build the confidence and find the courage to be unapologetically proud of who you are.

Becoming invites you to see others as they are, not how you want them to be.

Becoming invites you to fight the fear and feel the freedom.

Becoming invites you to love yourself unconditionally and without hesitation.

My parting wish for you is that you meet *yourself* sooner so you can love *yourself* longer.

ACKNOWLEDGMENTS

As I reflect on everything and everyone that contributed to the writing of this book, I'm overwhelmed – with gratitude. Sure, there were plenty of times throughout this process I was completely overwhelmed, but as I near the end of the effort, that's not what sticks with me. It's not all the hard work. It's not the countless hours. It's not even the steady stream of tears. What remains are the people. I will forever remember the relentless support and assistance I received. The unconditional love and encouragement gifted to me will forever remain in my heart.

I'm inclined to say that this book would have never existed without my coach, editor, and publisher, Demi at Year of the Book Press. If I'd magically managed to complete it without her, it would've been considerably harder, it would've taken substantially longer, and it wouldn't be nearly as good. Demi, thank you for teaching me how to trust you, trust the process and, most of all, trust myself. Thank you for your beautiful balance of patience and persistence as you expertly motivated me on this grueling journey. Thank you for your commitment and enthusiasm on every call and in every message. Thank you for deeply caring about me and my story. Thank you for believing in me and for exceeding my expectations every step of the way.

This book is a lifetime in the making, and yet, may never have been written without the considerable support and encouragement of so many kind, caring, and compassionate people. Countless people from all walks of life, each with their own beautiful and unique story, generously poured into me over the last seven years. The clarity they helped me find and the confidence they helped me build are the lens through which this book was written. From the bottom of my heart and the depths of my soul, thank you all... you know who you are.

To the institutions and organizations who welcomed me to share my story, thank you for the opportunity.

To the audiences who listened to me speak, thank you for your attention.

To the individuals who invited me to be their coach, thank you for your trust.

To the person holding this book, thank you for reading.

ABOUT THE AUTHOR

Don Mamone's decade-long career in hospitality culminated with their role as the Director of Events at the prestigious Beverly Hilton. Determined to embrace their creativity and pursue the dream of entrepreneurship, Don and their wife Emily opened a photography studio, The Mamones LLC, and have exceeded the expectations for their loyal clients from Dallas to destinations around the world for over fifteen years.

As a keynote speaker and identity coach, Don teaches audiences and clients how to reach their maximum potential and impact by discovering and embracing their true identity. Don is a committed advocate for the LGBTQIA2S+ community and consults with companies and organizations dedicated to diversity, inclusivity, and representation as well as creating safe spaces that support and encourage unapologetic authenticity.

When not traveling the world for creative projects and speeches, Don lives happily outside the gender binary in Dallas with their talented spouse Emily and their creative child Frankie.

To book Don for a speaking engagement
or for coaching and consulting services
visit **donmamone.com**

www.ingramcontent.com/pod-product-compliance
Lightning Source LLC
Chambersburg PA
CBHW060601080526
44585CB00013B/643